# "What
Does
Joan
Say?"

# "What Does Joan Say?"

## My Seven Years
## as White House Astrologer
## to Nancy and Ronald Reagan

By Joan Quigley

A BIRCH LANE PRESS BOOK
Published by Carol Publishing Group

A Birch Lane Press Book
Published by Carol Publishing Group

Editorial Offices
600 Madison Avenue
New York, NY 10022

Sales & Distribution Offices
120 Enterprise Avenue
Secaucus, NJ 07094

In Canada: Musson Book Company
A division of General Publishing Co. Limited
Don Mills, Ontario

ISBN 1-55972-032-8

Manufactured in the United States of America

10  9  8  7  6  5  4  3  2  1

Library of Congress Cataloging-in-Publication Data

Quigley, Joan.
    What does Joan say? : my seven years as White House astrologer to
Nancy and Ronald Reagan / by Joan Quigley.
      p.  cm.
    ISBN 1-55972-032-8 : $17.95
    Includes index.
    1. Reagan, Ronald--Friends and associates. 2. Reagan, Nancy,
1923--Friends and associates. 3. Quigley, Joan. 4. Astrology and
politics. 5. United States--Politics and government--1981-1989.
I. Title.
E877.2.Q54  1990
973.9270922--dc20
                                                            90-31193
                                                            CIP

As might be expected, I read *My Turn* with more hindsight and also with a greater sense of anticipation than most readers will bring to it. I was pleased to note, then, that Mrs. Reagan has confirmed the accuracy of every important point in my book, *For the Record*. Where we differ in our versions of events, it is often though not always a matter of interpretation.

What she cannot understand is why I did it—that is, why I revealed that the President's schedule and therefore his life and the most important business of the American nation was largely under the control of the First Lady's astrologer. Frankly, I hesitated before putting this astounding fact into the historical record. I certainly did not "take this information . . . and twist it to seek . . . revenge."

The fact is, I wrote about astrology because it was an essential truth about the way the Reagans operated.

My description of White House life in my period as chief of staff would have made little sense if I had omitted it. All those schedule changes, when laid out in black on white pages, would have looked downright senseless in the absence of an explanation.

Would that there had been some other explanation—but there wasn't. Astrology was it. It was a daily, sometimes hourly, factor in every decision affecting the President's schedule. Nancy Reagan says "unequivocally" that "Joan (Quigley)'s recommendations had nothing to do with policy or politics—ever. Her advice was confined to . . . Ronnie's schedule, and to what days were good or bad. . . ."

But he—or in this case she—who controls the President's schedule controls the workings of the presidency. It is the national chart of influence.

Although using an astrologer "never struck (her) as particularly strange," she concealed her consultations from her husband, the staff (with the exception of Michael Deaver and, later, Bill Henkel and me), and the Secret Service.

What a shock it must have been to the agents, who so carefully guarded the President, to learn that a total stranger—to them—knew not only intimate details of presidential movements, but could actually set the time of these moves! Surely they would think that posed a security risk. In retrospect, I think the nation owes Ms. Quigley a vote of gratitude. She really seems to have been interested in nothing but astrology. "Nobody was hurt by it—except, possibly, me," writes Mrs. Reagan.

—From a review of Nancy Reagan's *My Turn* by Donald Regan, Ronald Reagan's chief of staff, which appeared in the *Washingtonian*, December, 1989. Reprinted with permission of the *Washingtonian*.

# Contents

7

# "What Does Joan Say?"

# I
# Author to Reader

This is a book I never thought I'd write. In May of 1988 when Donald Regan's book came out, causing such an uproar, I rejected all suggestions that I document my Reagan years. I said as little as was possible to the media. I tried above all to keep from damaging the President I had admired and served for seven years with total dedication.

Now Nancy's book, *My Turn*, has forced me to reconsider. It reads like fiction and much of it is evasive. What she has left out about the way she used astrology and my ideas would fill a book. I now feel it is appropriate for me to write one.

Normally, I keep silent about my professional work. However, in late May 1987, Nancy Reagan said to me, "Joan, you have been a very important part of this administration." Nancy had put into words what I already knew: that I had contributed ideas and astrological advice that shaped administration policy with the U.S.S.R. and with regard to other crucial matters.

Through Nancy, I had a direct line to the President. That the astrological work I did for both Reagans affected the top level of government is now a matter of history. This book will describe what I did as an astrologer for seven years of the Reagan administration.

I was responsible for timing all press conferences, most speeches, the State of the Union addresses, the takeoffs and landings of Air Force One. I picked the time of Ronald Reagan's debate with Carter and the two debates with Walter Mondale; all extended trips abroad as well as the shorter trips and one-day excursions, the announcement that Reagan would run for a second term, briefings for all the summits except Moscow, although I selected the time to begin the Moscow trip. I timed congressional arm-twisting, the second Inaugural Oath of Office, the announcement of Anthony Kennedy's Supreme Court nomination. I delayed President Reagan's first operation for cancer from July 10, 1985, to July 13, and chose the time for Nancy's mastectomy.

I re-created Nancy's image, defused Bitburg, erected a chart for the INF Treaty. During Irangate, I sided with Nancy against Donald Regan's proposal to have the President go on the road to defend his policies one week after his second operation for cancer. I exposed the President as little as possible to the public and the media from January to August 1987, to protect him from both the physical and political dangers I foresaw.

I was heavily involved in what happened in the relations between the superpowers, changing Ronald Reagan's "Evil Empire" attitude, so that he went to Geneva prepared to meet a different kind of Russian leader and one he could convince of doing things our way. Improved relations, *glasnost* and *perestroika* may, in some small measure, have come out of this.

During this seven-year period, I read the President's horoscope often hourly, for political reasons as well as for safety.

Ronald Reagan is the first president elected in a zero year to survive his terms of office since William Henry Harrison died after a month in office on April 4, 1841.

In *For the Record*, Donald Regan referred to me as a clairvoyant. Clairvoyants are mystics or psychics.

I base my astrological analysis on the data provided by astronomers and charts calculated by computers. My conclusions are based on this accurate scientific material in the same way your doctor supports his diagnosis by the laboratory reports or an economist bases his predictions on statistics.

I do not gaze into crystal balls. I study many different kinds of charts and come to well-thought-out conclusions.

When the word "astrology" is mentioned, most people think of Sun Sign columns in newspapers. Sun Sign columns are harmless and amusing, but they are incomplete. Many of them are not even written by astrologers. A person must be very credulous indeed to believe that the same thing is happening to one twelfth of the world's population during a given day or month. I have never written Sun Sign columns even when it would have been profitable financially for me to do so.

Many people scoff when the word "scientific" is used in connection with astrology because of these Sun Sign columns and because people who call themselves astrologers make outrageous prophecies, tongue in cheek, for tabloids or sensational magazines, to entertain their readers.

My predictions, on the other hand, are made in plain language, well in advance, on national TV, and usually what I predict happens.

One of the reasons I am writing this book is that modern astrology is so generally misunderstood, even among uninformed believers.

In the days following the Regan revelation, the fact that the Reagans had used astrology was ridiculed and made into a political liability. A kind of circus atmosphere prevailed, with imposters from all over the country claiming to have done what I had done.

Partially this is because anyone who wishes to can call himself or herself an astrologer. There are at present no enforced standards for astrologers. Qualifying tests are optional. Unworthy people cannot be prevented from assuming what should be a respected title. It is deplorable!

How did this come about? Why has a discipline that dates back to the beginning of civilization been so dishonored and discredited? Partially it is because of the "Pop" astrologer. These people dealing only in Sun Signs are, for the most part, entertainers and clever showmen. They have always existed. The Bible inveighs against them.

However, the Bible praises astrology in other places. The Biblical prophets were astrologers. In the 53rd chapter of the Book of Isaiah, the prophet, who was an astrologer, describes the life of Jesus 600 years before His birth. In the more literal translation of the New Testament currently used in Catholic churches, the Wise Men of the King James version are described as astrologers.

Archaeologists and geologists are now beginning to theorize that Moses' "pillar of fire" was a volcanic eruption, and the parting of the waters of the Red Sea, a tidal wave, which suggests to me that Moses may have been a skilled mundane astrologer, who chose the time of the Exodus deliberately. For it is common knowledge that the Jews learned astrology during their sojourn in Egypt. Nor were astrologers strangers in Greece and Rome.

One of the most famous passages in Ecclesiastes states, "To every thing there is a season, and a time to every purpose under heaven." These included a time to be born, a time for planting or reaping, and so forth.

Time and location are the two most important elements in

astrology. An astrological chart is made up of the configurations of the Sun, Moon and planets in relation to a particular spot on earth at a particular time. The most basic form of astrological chart is the horoscope, or birth chart. This describes the health, character and destiny of an individual during his lifetime. The horoscope is calculated for the moment the baby cries and takes his first breath.

As a person grows older, his state of mind and situation change or progress; his physical body develops and grows and declines. The astrologer can predict these changes. The astrologer—and this is of very great importance—must also take into consideration the current movements of the planets that indicate the outside influences affecting the individual, rather like the weather conditions of life.

In addition to birth charts, there are charts for the beginning of events. When a meeting takes place, an important document is signed, a journey begins, the astrologer can warn you about avoidable dangers and tell you how something potentially good can be made even better yet. He can predict whether a venture will end in failure or success.

In some cases, such charts must be very exact because of technical factors. For example, the announcement of Anthony Kennedy's nomination to the Supreme Court was timed with a stopwatch, not only to the minute but to the exact second of time. In other cases, being off a few minutes is not of great importance. However, a horoscope of birth must always be exact to the second for predictions of major importance to be correct.

Looking at the chart of a beginning, an astrologer translates the symbols of the planets and signs and degrees of the Zodiac in which they are found, to give a word picture of the event. The astrologer must put into words a description of each chart.

This is always done by combining the chart of an individual with the chart of an event. For instance, a chart for the President's beginning something would not work equally well for somebody else. The chart of President Reagan's declaring that he would run for a second term had to be in sync with his own horoscope. Had Walter Mondale chosen the same announcement time, it wouldn't necessarily have enabled him to win.

Location is also of utmost importance. I have a method for choosing a particular location at a given time period to achieve desirable results. For instance, President Reagan's location chart for the second week in October 1986 in Reykjavik, Iceland, was entirely different from the chart for that same period in Washington, D.C. In Reykjavik, he would attract global attention; in Washington, rather an average week.

Astrology was conceived in pre-history. It developed in the cradle of civilization, the fertile crescent—Chaldea, Babylon, Assyria, Judea and Egypt—where it grew and prospered.

I never really understood why astrology began in that area until one midnight, during a visit to Egypt, I stood before the beautiful allée of sculptured rams that leads into the Temple of Karnak near Thebes. Looking up, I saw above me the white shadow of the Milky Way diluted by moonlight, while showers and clusters of stars of the most brilliant intensity studded the vast, sensuous softness of the rich, lush blue-black sky.

The next day, we crossed over to the Valley of the Kings, where Tutankhamen was entombed within opulent walls decorated by frescos of the ancient Egyptian Zodiacal symbols under an arched deep-blue ceiling painted with stars.

In Egypt, you have to be aware of the heavens at night. I have never seen a more spectacular night sky anywhere. It is no wonder that the ancients in that part of the world were conscious of stars. And the observant ones must have noticed the correspondence between what was happening in the heavens and what took place on earth. Perhaps they began by remarking on how the Moon influenced the tides and the lunar and solar cycles affected agriculture and then progressed to the planets and later to the stars.

From antiquity into the Middle Ages, through the Renaissance into the 17th century, astrology flourished. Kings, queens, popes, great generals, wealthy princes consulted astrologers. Every court had one.

Astrologers were the wise men, the educated men, the early scientists, the thinkers. They could see into the future. They taught the young boys who would grow up to be their masters. They encouraged and advised great men of action.

They lived, however, at the mercy of the powerful. Although they were in some cases the spiritual and intellectual superiors of those in power, they, like so many great artists and musicians, were regarded as dependents.

Theirs was often a precarious existence. When they were lucky enough to promise good things that happened, there were honors and rewards. But with every downturn of their ruler's fortunes, dared they predict them, there was the risk of execution or banishment or prison.

In the beginning, the modern roles of astrology and astronomy were reversed. The early astrologers were astronomers who observed and calculated the positions and configurations of the Sun, Moon, planets and more distant stars only so that they would be able to interpret and predict. Astronomy was the astrologer's tool, nothing more. Astrologers not only forecast the future, they compiled the entire psychological knowledge of antiquity as well.

The early astrologers, however, never cast the horoscopes of ordinary people. They directed their efforts to the charts of rulers and conquerors in which the destinies of their realms and armies and all of their subjects were to be seen. They compared their rulers' horoscopes with those of their enemies to see who would triumph. They cast up charts of the location of the kingdom so as to predict what would happen to crops and whether to expect natural disasters or plagues. In all these ways, they were the precursors of all modern political astrologers.

Two of the greatest scientists who ever lived, Albert Einstein and Sir Isaac Newton, believed in astrology. You have only to read this quote from Einstein to know that he believed:

> Everything is determined, the beginning as well as the end, by forces over which we have no control. It is determined for the insect as well as the star. Human beings, vegetables, our cosmic dust, all dance to a mysterious tune intoned in the distance by an invisible player.

During a discussion with the noted astronomer Edmund Halley, who was arguing against astrology, Sir Isaac Newton replied, "The difference between you and me, Mr. Halley, is that I have studied the subject and you have not."

Indeed, many of Sir Isaac's early 18th-century contemporaries were astrology's detractors. These early academic scientists pointed out that things were happening in people's lives that astrologers were unable to account for or predict.

This was because Uranus, Neptune and Pluto, the more remote and slower moving planets that have so much to do with modern life, hadn't been discovered yet by astronomers. Uranus was discovered at the end of the 18th century, Neptune in the middle of the 19th and Pluto in 1930. After astrologers had had time to study the effects of these three planets, they were able to attribute to them what had hitherto been unexplained by the five planets known from ancient times.

How baffled the early astrologers must have been when they could not account for the deceptions, rumors and drug or alcohol abuse caused by Neptune, or the overnight success or sudden collapse of fortune so typical of Uranus. Neptune and Pluto together in the air sign of Gemini were responsible for the miracle of flight in the early 1900s, and Pluto rules, among other things, that uniquely 20th-century phenomenon, the media. And each new discovery coincided with an expanded human awareness and the innovations that transformed human life-styles.

Having devoted the better portion of my life to the study and practice of astrology, I am convinced of its scientific merit. I graduated from Vassar with honors. I have a knowledge of history and many of the great horoscopes of history. It is my fervent wish that one day astrology will again take its proper place among other respected disciplines in the scientific community.

In this spirit, I dedicate this book to Astrology.

# II

# Nancy's Image

In early May 1988, Donald Regan revealed in his book *For the Record* that Nancy Reagan had "absolute faith in a woman astrologer in San Francisco." And the media soon found out that Nancy had consulted me about the President's horoscope. During the seven years I served the administration professionally, I kept silent. Of course, my immediate family could not help being aware of Nancy's constant phone calls, but I never discussed these calls and they never mentioned them.

Certain people at the White House of necessity had to know that Nancy was using astrology. However, only a few insiders were actually aware that I was the astrologer.

When the news broke, I was in Paris, my last stop after a Mediterranean cruise. My sister phoned from San Francisco the night of my arrival and told me that a reporter from the *Chronicle* had called and asked her if she believed in astrology.

Ruth said, "Of course! As you know, my sister is a well-known astrologer."

The reporter then said that the *San Francisco Chronicle* had published the report that the Reagans had used astrology during his presidency. She added that the article was on the next-to-last page of the news section.

When the reporter asked for my phone number in Paris, my sister gave the number on the itinerary, which fortunately was incorrect. This gave Ruth time to read the inconspicuously placed article. She called me immediately. Consequently, I was forewarned when the reporter finally reached my Paris hotel and demanded to know if I was the astrologer mentioned in the Regan book. Despite her continued insistence, I refused to comment, either to confirm or to deny. The hotel operator interrupted with another long distance call. It was Nancy. We talked for about twenty minutes. She praised the way Ruth had handled the situation and said that she would be in touch with me when I arrived home.

Later, Ruth told me that Nancy had called her and said, "This must never come out!"

"Not while you are in office," Ruth said, "but what about after you are out of office?"

"Never," said Nancy. "It must never come out!" And then she realized that she was after all speaking to my sister. She temporized, "Well, I guess I'm like Scarlett O'Hara. I'll think about that some other time."

The following night, Ruth called to tell me that astrologers all over the country, both male and female, were claiming that they were the one Regan had mentioned.

The next morning, I took the Concorde to New York. After spending the night at an airport hotel, I was intercepted as I was about to board a plane to San Francisco by a young reporter from *Time* magazine. He told me he had booked a seat on the plane at the last moment for the purpose of interviewing me. I decided to grant him the first interview. Having been alerted in Paris, I was prepared.

Nancy called me the night I arrived home. She spent forty minutes on the telephone trying to persuade me not to say anything to the media. She reminded me that the President just put his hand up and refused to talk to reporters when he didn't want to. She told me to deal that way with the media.

I told her firmly that I was not going to do that. I reminded her that she would have had a very hard time, if not an impossible one, to find anyone who would have remained silent for seven years about work of such magnitude.

She said she knew that. Someone at the White House had leaked my name to the media. She knew who it was but could not do anything about it because of the person's importance. However, she continued to insist that I say nothing at all.

I said, "Nancy, I can't do that. I am a reputable astrologer. Charlatans and impostors from all over the country are making false claims. I am determined to show who and what I am and represent reputable astrologers honorably. I will in no way injure you. But I will not refuse to be interviewed."

When she finally realized that, for the moment, she would have to give up, she said, "I guess I have my answer."

Half thinking aloud, I said, "But what will I do if someone asks about sensitive matters?"

Nancy said, "Lie if you have to. If you have to, lie." Nancy never called again. After seven years of being constantly in touch, after communicating continually during the last three months of the 1980 campaign, the last word Nancy ever said to me was, "Lie!"

Almost from the time I first learned to read a horoscope, I knew that if one was given the ability to look into the future, one was also provided with the wisdom to know what and what not to say. And so, when asked about my work for the Reagans, I did not lie. I followed my own standards. I said only what I wanted to say. When it was inappropriate to comment, I simply said nothing.

When the news broke, Nancy told the media that she consulted me because after the assassination attempt, she was naturally concerned about the President's safety. But she had another concern, one which was of almost equal importance to her. At least, that was my impression at the end of April in 1981 when she phoned for the first time since mid-January.

This was a time when the President was very popular and even the normally critical media had little to say against him. During this period, he was winning over the opposition in Congress with the very greatest diplomacy and charm. However, despite the smooth and effective operation of his White House staff and the excellence of his cabinet, no one had managed to solve, in even the most primitive way, the problem of Nancy's image.

Nancy was being pilloried by the press. From the White House china she planned to buy to her expensive clothes, her every movement was ridiculed and criticized. Every word she said brought on more public disapproval, every probe into her past resulted in a new round of spitefulness and scandal. It was not only embarrassing, it was ironic that the President's wife, who had helped bring about her husband's success, was now his only political liability.

I was amused to learn when I was watching the 1988 Republican Convention on television that someone had been putting about the rumor that Michael Deaver had been the architect of Nancy's image. That her image had had to have an architect was, of course, obvious to everyone. And from time to time, it had been mentioned. When the change in her image began to be noticed, she attributed it to members of her staff so as to mention the "new" Nancy and at the same time dismiss the change by giving the credit for what was being done to someone insignificant. It was obviously a ploy. It should be equally obvious to everyone that the change in image could not have come from Michael Deaver.

Michael Deaver began working in the White House in December 1980. He supervised Nancy's staff during the period her image was at its worst and the only sour note in an administration that was otherwise popular, not only in Washington but in the rest of the country as well. Michael Deaver, like all the other Reagan aides, hadn't the slightest idea what to do or he would already have done it.

One of the reasons Nancy asked if she could consult me about the President's horoscope in late April of 1981, was that she knew from her own experience during the '80 campaign that my work was utterly reliable and that I could solve problems and avoid difficulties. Also, she felt comfortable because I knew the world quite well and understood people and how they functioned and interacted with one another, not to mention my knowledge of history and grasp of politics.

This is what she said that day. I remember it verbatim. First, she asked, "Could you have told about the assassination attempt?"

"Yes, of course I could had I been looking. However, I haven't been following your charts or tracking the mundane material for Washington. I'm sorry. Had I been looking, I would have warned you."

She then said, "I'm getting a terrible press. It's so unfair. I'm really a very nice person. Can you tell me what to do? I'm willing to pay you."

I told her I would like to have time to think about it and asked her to call back in a few days.

Whether to take on the responsibility of becoming the astrologer to the President and the First Lady required serious thought. I had to consider that the President's horoscope indicated that he was vulnerable to assassination. To protect him effectively was practically a full-time job for several astrologers. Later in this book, I will detail the number and complexity of the charts that had to be analyzed and compared with the President's to be absolutely certain that my work was fail-safe.

It was an especially difficult task, as there was, of course, the zero-year phenomenon. It is a matter of record that every president elected in a year ending in zero beginning with William Henry Harrison had died in office. I knew from having studied his chart that Ronald Reagan would not die of natural causes during his term in office. But I also had to be sure if I took on the difficult assignment of using my astrological expertise to protect the President, that it was possible to do so.

Let me explain the astrological basis for these occurrences. Every 19.85 years, the major planets Jupiter and Saturn make a conjunction. The first of the most recent series of these conjunctions in earth signs fell on January 26, 1842, in Capricorn. This was known as the Great Mutation. Subsequent conjunctions all produced the same result. Even the rotational Jupiter-Saturn conjunction, which fell in a water sign rather than the earth sign typical of this series, coincided with Warren Harding's term in office, which like the others was cut short by his death. The water sign was Scorpio, the sign of death, and so it was to be expected that a death would result.

In 1981, there was another rotational conjunction, this one in the air sign of Libra. Most astrologers at the time were shaking their heads in anticipation of another death in office, but I said that an air sign conjunction, while dangerous, was less fatalistic and that Reagan had a chance of surviving two terms in office. Protecting his safety would not be easy, but it was possible, in my opinion.

I am always being asked about my intuitions, feelings or hunches, as if I could make astrological predictions off the top of my head or by gazing into some sort of crystal ball or reading frogs' entrails. How little people realize the tough, intricate, complex, demanding work that goes into the kind of astrology I practice. I had to work at my discipline conscientiously for many years to reach the level of competence that would enable me to undertake such a demanding task. At that point, I had the

knowledge, the experience, the resourcefullness and the willingness to take the infinite pains that were needed to guide Ronald
Reagan safely from May of 1981 until June 1 of his last year in
office, when his own horoscope indicated that his life would no
longer be in danger. I knew that if I succeeded in protecting
him, he would go out of office one of the most popular presidents in United States history. He would be the first since 1840
to survive two terms in office after being elected in a zero year.

In addition, I knew that the Reagans' horoscopes would be
uppermost in my mind during that seven-year period almost to
the exclusion of anything else, that I would be held to absolute
standards of performance, that I had to be right. I would have to
put my career and my personal life virtually on hold during that
period. I would have to do what I believe few other astrologers
would have consented to do: to say nothing to anyone about
doing work of such importance and which, had it been known, it
would have so greatly enhanced my reputation during that
period. I knew, however that my silence was imperative. Had
my work been known, the questioning on the part of the media
would have been counterproductive. As an insider, it would be
inappropriate for me to predict freely about such public figures
as the Reagans when I, a nationally known astrologer, would be
asked to do so. As it turned out, I made only the most perfunctory comments, nothing that would endanger the President.

I also knew that the President, who runs what amounts to the
largest entity in the world today, the United States government,
is paid only a fraction of the salary and other financial benefits of
the head of a big corporation. The Reagans did not have vast
wealth. Nancy offered to pay me, yes. But I had to know that
even if she wished to, she could not afford to pay me even a
fraction of what I was worth. I could not have done this for the
Reagans had I not had other sources of income.

Nancy knew exactly what she would be getting. She was far
too intelligent not to be well aware of what she could expect.

And I imagine she congratulated herself often, during the seven years of the presidency that she consulted me, on having found an incredible bargain.

I knew that if I decided to take the Reagans on, I would be giving up my time and effort like all those who take part in any administration, sacrificing the rewards they command in the private sector in order to serve their country. I was aware, however, that unlike them, I would not have the prestige they had while serving. I also knew that I could expect no gratitude from Nancy. After donating my astrological expertise to the 1980 campaign, after being constantly in touch by phone during the crucial last three months and doing all the pivotal things I will discuss in a later chapter, she had not written so much as a perfunctory thank-you note. I knew I could expect nothing from Nancy other than the token sum I would ask and she would agree to pay.

Yet the temptation to say "Yes" was very great. There was also the satisfaction of working well with someone. And Nancy and I did work well together. Often we began our sessions with pleasantries or brief discussions about some current political situation. But ours were working sessions. They often lasted up to two hours of total concentration at both ends of the phone.

In many ways, Nancy was an ideal client. She trusted me completely and followed my advice absolutely. Yet, as we worked, she combined her areas of knowledge and her usually excellent political judgment with my astrological expertise. The combination was for a time unbeatable. During that time when I considered whether to accept Nancy's request, I felt that working with Nancy was a plus.

Most important, however, I felt that doing astrology for a president would be a unique experience, insofar as we know, in American history. My family and I have always been devoted patriots. But patriotism aside, I realized that this was no 19th-century president, but the leader of the most powerful nation and the free world. In fact, the world's most powerful man for the first eight years of the 1980s. I would be able to contribute to, protect and, at times, to influence this most powerful man. I would participate in a more intimate way than the publicly recognized insiders of greatest importance. It was bound to be an incomparable and fascinating experience.

Three days later, when Nancy called, I told her I would do the President's astrology as well as her own and that, given time, I would be able to transform her image from undesirable to enviable. She arranged to pay me by putting her own money into the bank account of a friend, who then sent me a check for the amount I billed Nancy each month. Nancy really wanted me to do her astrology desperately enough to be willing to spend her own money. And she felt that the fact that she spent any money at all repaid me fully.

"I want everyone to love me" were Nancy's first words after I agreed to work with her on a professional basis. I had to smile, the words were so typical of a person with her kind of horoscope.

This is the situation I had to deal with when I took over the creation of a new image for Nancy in May of 1981:

> *San Francisco Chronicle*, December 7, 1980: Nancy Reagan had never set foot in Sacramento until her husband became Governor—she was horrified by what she found. She spoke scornfully of her forced residence in Sacramento. "Thank heavens we can escape to Beverly Hills on the weekends," she told a journalist, adding that she had to go to Beverly Hills at least once a week to have her hair done. "No one in Sacramento can do hair."

> *San Francisco Chronicle*, December 16, 1980: Last week, Washington sources said Reagan aides had dropped broad hints that Mrs. Reagan wanted the Carters to move

into Blair House so White House redecorating could begin.

Mrs. Reagan's aides denied the report. But they said she might decide to move out of the White House early when her husband's presidency is over to allow the next first lady to get a head start.

*San Francisco Sunday Examiner & Chronicle*, "Scene," December 21, 1980: Headline: THE NEXT FIRST LADY AND HER "WALKER."

"Jerry Zipkin," says *Women's Wear Daily*, "is a perennial bachelor who entertains and escorts rich women with busy husbands. Zipkin has been walking Nancy for about fifteen years now. He squires her to Monsieur Marc, her New York hairdresser; he takes her shopping for couturier clothes on Seventh Avenue in New York . . . and to cozy, chatty lunches and suppers."

Gossip columnist Maxine Cheshire, quoting an acquaintance of Nancy Reagan's, says that the favorite pastime of the president-elect's wife is lunching with Zipkin at Le Bistro in Los Angeles "listening to him gossip about everyone they know."

These "Let them eat cake" reports were followed by a March 2, 1981, article in the *San Francisco Chronicle* headlined: "NANCY SAYS THE PRESS IS MEAN."

Nancy Reagan said in an interview published yesterday that the press has "made me sound terrible—I never got half a chance" to make a good impression on the American people.

"They make me sound so terrible. And it started before I even got there. They wrote things that were so—so unbelievable."

She cited as an example a story that in her zeal for interior decoration, she had suggested taking down a wall in the Lincoln bedroom.

"They knew none of those things were true," she said. "But they went ahead and printed them anyway. It was pretty mean."

In all fairness, I must credit Nancy with attributes other than the ones already mentioned. She was very protective of the President. She was almost psychic in her awareness of his best interests and the motives of those surrounding him. Her ability to win over important people and her handling of complex situations had provided backing that had been indispensable to his achieving the highest office. She was well organized. She was an accomplished hostess and indisputably the most sophisticated and glamorous woman to occupy the position of First Lady since Jackie.

That was part of Nancy's problem. She expected to be treated like Jackie. But the United States in 1980 in no way resembled the United States in 1960. The state of the union and the mood of the country were as unalike as Nancy and Jackie, who despite certain superficial similarities, were very different women.

Jackie was totally disinterested in politics and couldn't have cared less about her husband becoming president. In fact, she quite emphatically didn't want it. She participated in the campaign grudgingly and appeared in public only when she was forced to. But Papa Joe Kennedy was much too ambitious for his son and far too shrewd to allow Jackie to detract from Jack Kennedy's popularity. He was willing to do what he had to. So he hired Madison Avenue brains to create a desirable image for an all but recalcitrant Jackie. It was even rumored that he had to bribe her. But he had the money to spend, and he knew where to go. He wasn't a successful, self-made man for no reason. And

as it turned out, what began as a well
campaign snowballed into a publicity

Jackie herself made very little eff
for her to be dressed by the best F
by great hairdressers. Her face was pi
iarity turned her good looks into radiant bea
appealing young children, the good schools and a
the socially prominent, affluent background and, top
her handsome young president husband combined to
Jackie her place in a kind of fairy tale latter-day Camelot uniqu
in the history of the republic. Madison Avenue had struck just
the right chord in the national consciousness of the early '60s.
The public wanted someone to worship and idolize, someone
they could adore like royalty. The adulation Jackie received has
never been equaled.

Yet aside from obliging the photographers and supervising
her children and cooperating with Clement Conger, who taste-
fully refurbished the White House, Jackie habitually shirked the
more tedious duties of the First Lady. I remember in 1962
reading in *The New York Times* that Jackie, pleading illness, had
failed to appear one morning to greet a delegation of Girl Scouts
visiting the White House. By evening, however, she recovered
in time to hostess a ball attended by André Malraux and other
exciting celebrities. Nor did she appear to accept the traditional
bottles of perfume the Senators' wives present to the President's
wife annually. That was the way things were in the early '60s.
People wanted to believe in heroes and heroines.

The morning of January 20, 1981, even as Ronald Reagan was
taking the oath of office for the first term of the presidency,
public attention was diverted from the event by media coverage
of the return of the hostages. The hostages' long imprisonment
at the American Embassy in Iran had been a national ordeal that

d received almost total attention from Carter and the media
or months, and it had resulted in a general spirit of malaise and
discouragement. The United States had lost respect abroad and
a great many Americans no longer took pride in their country.
The low ebb of patriotism, the economic disasters of
double-digit interest rates and galloping inflation were equaled
only by high unemployment figures. People who had lost their
jobs were helpless to cope with the poverty afflicting their
families. In this atmosphere, it was not only unlikely but unrealistic for a First Lady to expect to be treated as Jackie had
been in the affluent early '60s, following as they did the relatively untroubled and prosperous Eisenhower era.

This is the reasoning that went into the solution I proposed to
Nancy. I had known Nancy Reagan during the years the
Reagans were in between the California governorship and
Ronnie's attempt to win the 1976 Republican nomination for
president, which, while it failed, increased the attention they
received and brought back all the fair-weather friends who
temporarily had deserted them, as well as attracting new, even
more important ones. It marked the beginning of their successful climb to the White House. I remember that during the in-
between period I've described, Nancy complained of having few
real friends and being pinched for money, although they had the
house in Pacific Palisades and the Santa Barbara ranch and some
income, despite Ronnie's reduced earning capacity.

I think it meant a lot to her to be an accepted member of a
group that was privileged, exclusive and snobbish, and she
valued all her superficial status symbols and having the means to
spend extravagantly. Unlike so many of the women she admired, Nancy had never been able to have really big money.

Keeping all this in mind, one can see why, when Ronnie was
elected President, Nancy felt that as First Lady she had
achieved the ultimate in social position—except perhaps for
Queen Elizabeth II, whose hereditary throne and wealth

granted her the only rank superior to her own in Nancy's personal pecking order. She had also planned to be the darling of American designer fashion and to be featured in all the most stylish magazines.

In 1981, Nancy met the Queen of England for the first time. It was decided that she should not curtsy as a matter of policy. Personally, I think it must have killed her. She was always very impressed by British royalty. Whenever she had Charles in tow or Princess Di, she would name-drop. She said she liked Fergie because she was down to earth. And she really liked to mention Queen Elizabeth.

One really funny thing she told me about a later trip concerned having breakfast with Queen Elizabeth and Philip. I think it was at Balmoral. Nancy had had visions of a real English country breakfast, with the silver salvers filled with bacon and eggs and sausages, the kippered herring and so forth. She was really surprised when all she was offered for breakfast was a package of American corn flakes.

I was always amused by her worshipful attitude toward royalty. But then, there are a lot of women in this country who would drink the tea that was dumped in the Boston Harbor if it meant being invited to curtsy to the Queen of England.

Nancy's first move on entering the White House was to order a set of expensive new china. It is true that for a sophisticated hostess, the china was very much needed, and even had the money not been raised privately, it was not so dear that a still very wealthy nation couldn't afford it for state dinners. But in times such as I have described, it was resented because the purchase of new, expensive china seemed inappropriate. The impression that the new china made was neither sympathetic nor appealing and seemed both extravagant and unessential to the average citizen.

Nor was Nancy herself—the image she presented publicly, her values and the people she surrounded herself with and her real attitude toward others—the least bit sympathetic. Yet she had all the outward attributes of a presentable public figure. She was fashionably thin. She dressed stylishly. She was well coiffed. And while she wasn't really beautiful, she was very attractive.

What to do? To me, it was obvious. In San Francisco, and this is also true in all the other big cities of the United States, not to mention smaller communities, there is a tradition of volunteering. The private sector provides help for those in need for a very great variety of reasons. And whether it is illness or poverty or drug addiction or lack of education or conflicts within families or any other crying need, whatever problem afflicts their fellow human beings, there are Americans in all walks of life who dedicate personal effort or talent or money or time to benefit the less fortunate. In this respect, the American people are more generous than those of any other nation in world history.

"I want everyone to love me," Nancy said. When Nancy spoke of being universally loved, I thought of Eleanor Roosevelt. Not that she didn't have detractors. However, a great many people loved Eleanor Roosevelt because of her sympathy and caring for others, which was so deep and sincere that even FDR's worst enemies, even those who called her a "do-gooder" and the "dupe of pinkos," had to admit that her feelings were real and her motives unselfish. She participated in an entirely different way from Nancy. She went places and responded to needs at a time when so many people were troubled and in want and desperate. In that way, she too was a working partner.

"I want everyone to love me!" The wish to be well thought of is natural and human. And a great deal of good is done because of it. That was my thought when I began to recreate Nancy's image. It is quite usual for women of wealth and social position to serve on the boards of charitable institutions, to help plan tax-deductible benefit parties or in some other way to help raise funds for worthy causes. Nancy's main interest was Ronnie's political career. She satisfied her desire for fulfillment and recognition through advancing his position. However, I knew that any woman with Nancy's social pretensions would have a pet charity, perhaps several.

I asked her, and the quite predictable answer was, "Yes, the Drug Rehabilitation Program and the Foster Grandparents Program." I told her that these two charities would be what she would be known for from now on, that she would talk about them whenever she granted interviews and make them her personal crusade. She must be a kind of ministering angel of mercy, a sort of super national mother figure. I told her to set her staff to ferreting out appealing letters from children, for instance, and make a point of answering them. Or she could respond to some needy person, making sure at the same time that the story would be well publicized in the media. She was to show how kind she was and how generous and how interested in simple people's problems and needs.

I told her she must play down all her privileged social connections and that her only publicized attendance at parties would be at official entertainments and events having to do with her duties as First Lady or her lectures or promotions for one of her charities. I warned her not to give the impression of being snobbish or exclusive, and while she should always be as well dressed and attractive as possible, she must avoid making a point of fashion and clothes.

I said there would be absolutely no articles in fashionable magazines, or at least no interviews granted to them. That was the hardest thing for her—to give that up. She tried to wheedle me into letting her do that, but I was firm. I think after her image improved, I allowed her one small interview in W or one of the others. But during the period when we were turning her image around, I was uncompromising in my determination to refuse all interviews in *Harper's Bazaar, Vogue, Town and Country, Women's Wear Daily* and W.

In this, as in everything of importance I did for the Reagans, I began with a concept or policy and implemented it by skillful often very creative, technical astrological work. First of all, I told Nancy that from that point on we would wait for a month or six weeks, during which there would be the least possible exposure to the media. This was intended to clear the air of all the unfavorable impressions. During this period, she was not to grant even one interview. I wanted to make a clean break, and then provide an interim between the old Nancy image and the new one I proposed to bring into being.

After the waiting period, I began very cautiously to allow her to grant interviews. As she was in a position to command the times she would grant them, I was able to select only superb times astrologically that insured a favorable outcome. Often when working for the Reagans, I had to choose less than perfect times in order to conform with political necessity. That was all right. Astrological perfection is almost never possible when you deal with the real world. However, these times I picked for Nancy were as nearly perfect as any I've done. I waited as long as necessary to have the best possible times.

Gradually, her image took a turn for the better. Within a year, she had a more favorable press. Her performance in late March of 1982 at the Gridiron Club Dinner was her way of making herself seem more human by poking fun at herself. It was her idea. It was a good one. It was a kind of culmination of all I had planned for her and the result of the control I'd exercised over her for her own good.

The following newspaper stories resulted from my overall policy and use of astrology. One can see how successfully Nancy's efforts were directed between early 1982 and late December of 1983.

2/16/82    Nancy Reagan Makes 2-Day Tour of Florida
           Drug Programs

| | |
|---|---|
| 2/17/82 | Nancy Reagan Plans to Step Up Efforts to Help Youth Drug Plans |
| 3/23/82 | Nancy Reagan Launches Anti-Drug Drive |
| 3/29/82 | Nancy Reagan Spoofs Herself at Gridiron Club Dinner |
| 4/24/82 | Nancy Reagan Names Advertising and Entertainment as Drug Villains |
| 6/5/82 | Nancy Reagan Visits Blind Children in Paris |
| 9/23/82 | Nancy Reagan Named Chairman Committee of Arts and Humanities |
| 4/16/83 | Child Who Had Liver Transplant Meets Reagans |
| 7/29/83 | Reagans Meet Viet Girl Adopted by US Family in 1973 |
| 10/13/83 | Nancy Reagan Blasts Entertainment Industry for Glamorizing Drugs |
| 11/14/83 | Reagans Transport Korean Children for Heart Surgery |
| 11/15/83 | Korean Children Visit White House Before Heart Surgery |
| 12/20/83 | Ahn Hi Sook and Lee Kil Woo are visited by Mrs. Reagan as they recover at St. Francis Hospital, Roslyn, NY. Illustration. Mrs. Reagan gives children and 15 others Cabbage Patch dolls, in short supply for holiday season. |

Quite typically, when Nancy thanked me for turning her image around, I said, and it was something she was already well aware of, "Nancy, Joe Kennedy paid between one and two million dollars in 1960 for what I have done for thousands in 1981. Really, you must admit it has been a present."

"I know," she said, "but you must realize I don't have that kind of money."

From Nancy's viewpoint, I was a kind of Pygmalion figure. I

created for her a beautiful, desirable image, hoping that in time she would grow into it and become the person I taught her to appear to be. I was also, as is so often the case in an astrologer-client relationship, like a teacher trying to focus a promising pupil's attention on a particular subject, to make learning a great adventure with undreamed of possibilities and rewards. And, like a teacher, I always kept a distance between us. At the end of every consultation, she would say in respectful tones, "Thank you."

Nancy followed the guidelines I'd laid down for her conscientiously and to the letter. She worked tirelessly and intelligently to achieve her goal of being admired and loved. By 1984, she had hit the top of polls of most-admired women and been showered with other honors. She had honorary degrees. She had been saluted for the drug program. She had her own hour-long TV special.

And I remember that at one point, when she had begun to think of herself not as an appendage of Ronnie but a power in her own right, I delivered a timely warning. One day she was enthusing about her undreamed of success. It was a heady realization, and I remember cautioning her, in her exhilaration at her own person, not to forget that the man who was responsible for her being First Lady needed special reassurances at such a time.

I told her she would be wise to redouble her efforts to please and encourage him, not because he was a jealous man, but because she was now shining in the spotlight. I advised her also to show twice as much as she ever had the full measure of her love, affection and appreciation. At that time, he would have been less than human not to have needed that. Her own mother could not have given her more perceptive or helpful advice. She probably wouldn't have thought of it. But a word to the wise was sufficient. I hadn't wasted my breath.

I was, however, disappointed in Nancy when I heard her

speech televised from the 1988 Republican Convention in Dallas. It was filled with thanks to those assembled for allowing her to experience being First Lady, for having had the chance to develop herself to the degree she had. Nowhere did she thank them for the priceless opportunity she had been given to contribute something to the country and the world.

Later, during an interview, a reporter asked her to tell him about the drug program, to give him an example of something she had found particularly touching in the course of her work. Her answer was, in effect, that there had been so very many, she couldn't single out any one case. I'm sure had they asked the President a comparable question, he would have responded with an anecdote about some example or incident that had really meant something to him.

My pupil was a consummate actress, but I couldn't help feeling that while she had worked hard and studied diligently, she had never really understood the reason for taking the course.

# III

# How Merv Griffin Introduced Me to Nancy Reagan

My years with Nancy and Ronald Reagan came about as the result of the astrological predictions I made for Merv Griffin. I was first asked to appear on the "Merv Griffin Show" in late April 1972. Merv's was then the most popular afternoon talk show in the country. I had done a lot of national and local TV shows, and except for a minute before I went on stage, I didn't feel the least bit nervous. I can't act my way out of a paper bag, but I can always comfortably discuss a subject I know as thoroughly as astrology.

The writer who conducted my pre-show interview gave me Merv's birth data and that of Merv's son, Tony. The first person who greeted me backstage when I arrived (I didn't catch his name or know his title) asked what I had seen in the Griffins' horoscopes. I told him that Merv had recently put money in Tony's name. It was true. After the show, that same man came to my dressing room to ask if I would do his horoscope as well as his family's. I said I couldn't. He turned out to be Merv's producer. I also refused to do Tony's mother's horoscope, so Merv was well aware from the beginning that I never did astrology for anyone unless I wanted to specifically.

Merv was born in San Mateo and brought up in the Bay Area. In the late '40s, he began his career as a singer for Freddy Martin's band. At that time, he had a marvelous romantic singing voice, but I don't think that was a very happy period in his life because he had so much potential to develop beyond the circumstances he began with. I knew him then from having gone dancing so frequently to Freddy Martin's music.

Meeting him again, for the first time on his show, I was as impressed with his speaking voice as I had once been with his singing voice. He was very suave, and, before the cameras, he couldn't have been friendlier. We talked and laughed during the commercial breaks. He gave a wonderful, sympathetic interview, the best and the nicest in the business.

I remember only two things about my predictions on that show, the first about Merv himself. I said his marriage would soon be breaking up. He shook his head in disbelief. Two weeks later, his wife served the divorce papers. Merv's horoscope was always easy for me to read. But he confided in me many times that I was the only one among the dozens of psychics and astrologers who appeared on his show who had ever told him anything about himself that actually happened.

The other prediction was one I saw but deliberately did not mention. It concerned President Richard Nixon. If you'll remember, in '72 he was reelected by a landslide. I saw the win. I also saw something that greatly disturbed me. A two-year horrendous configuration of the malefic planet Uranus to the most sensitive degree in his horoscope, beginning shortly before the election.

Uranus, at best, can be a king-maker. At worst, it is a throne-toppler. Classically, it removes something from a person's life that he values greatly. The damage Uranus causes can never be repaired, rather like a part of the body that has been removed surgically. Humpty Dumpty suffered a Uranus loss, and all the King's horses and men couldn't put Humpty back together ever. This is often true of broken relationships or the sudden unexpected losses that can be caused by adverse Uranus. A natural disaster also can result, but most typically the trouble is brought on by some person or persons turning against one. What I saw in Nixon's horoscope referred to the scandal known as "Watergate."

I can't be sure—it is so long ago—but I remember going on the "Merv Griffin Show" again the following December. That was when Merv began the pattern he always followed with me. First, he would ask me to list the predictions I'd made on the previous show that had come to pass. Then I would make my new predictions. He was always highly complimentary and, as time went on, gave me ever more glowing introductions.

In the summer of '73, I sent Merv a written report that was so accurate he sent me a handwritten letter, thanking me profusely. The next time I went on the show, he told me how right I'd been. Every electrical gadget in his home had gone out of whack just as I had predicted. He was even more impressed that I'd foretold events of a hallucinating day while he was traveling. I remember this, too, was unfavorable Uranus, the same planet that had been responsible for breaking up his marriage.

The current movements of important planets, such as Uranus, go back and forth and, quite typically, cause not just one but a series of aggravations. At that time, Uranus was afflicting Merv in all these ways. I was vaguely aware that the worst

Uranus affliction of his life was due in the early '90s. I'm usually too busy with the near future to look ahead that far. In 1973, the '90s seemed like another lifetime.

At any rate, shortly after I became a regular on the show, Merv told me that he shared a July 6th birthday and an interest in astrology with the governor of California's wife, Nancy Reagan. He had already mentioned me to her, and he asked my permission to have her call me.

I said yes. He gave Nancy my phone number in the summer of 1973. The rest is history. Literally.

The first time, Nancy consulted me mostly about personal problems. She had given me her exact birthtime, so doing her horoscope was easy. I remember I described to her in detail the matter she intended asking me about before she asked it. From the beginning, my accuracy impressed her. We always got along quite well. I knew the minute I cast up her chart that it was world-class. I told her I hadn't seen so superlative a stellium since Jackie's. I remember she asked what a "stellium" was, and I explained to her that it was a collection of planets in the same sign, or adjacent signs, very close together.

While there were ways in which Nancy's horoscope resembled Jackie's, they were not at all the same. I promised Nancy I would never publish her horoscope, and I am honoring that promise. From the standpoint of its being a historic and remarkable chart, it is a shame not to be able to describe it for posterity. However, so be it.

From then on, Nancy called every year or so for an update. Having seen Nancy's chart, I was very interested in Ronnie's horoscope because I knew that the world prominence shown in her chart would be intertwined with the destiny of her husband.

I had Nancy's birthtime to the minute, but to do Ronnie's chart was much more difficult because the Reagans did not know what time of day he was born, not even a hint. All Nancy could tell me was Ronnie's date and place of birth. No one who might have known was still alive, and no one remembered his late parents or other relatives mentioning his birthtime.

It was then I began painstakingly to rectify Ronald Reagan's horoscope. If you don't understand what "rectification" means, let me explain it. When you don't know what time of day an individual was born—and for serious astrology, the exact birthtime is indispensable—you must figure it out from such clues as the known events of that person's past, their appearance and psychological and physical characteristics not already explained by the other factors in the horoscope. In a difficult case, this can be argued many ways. With Ronnie, there were as many versions of his chart as there were interested astrologers. The process of rectification can take months, and the solution must be checked out mathematically.

In Ronnie's case, it was a long time before I was satisfied with my answer. Even for an experienced astrologer like me, rectifying Ronald Reagan's chart was laborious. In other cases, some very famous ones, I have been able to do it relatively fast. It all depends on the particular horoscope how hard or easy it will be. This process is rather like identifying a murderer from the clues available or solving a crossword puzzle by definitions. I know my rectification of Ronald Reagan's chart was a perfect one. It tested out over and over.

In the beginning, Nancy asked me if I would waive my fee. It is my policy never to do this. People tend not to value advice they don't have to pay for. I never charge, however, for spiritual advice.

I used a method on the Reagans' charts I've always found helpful with the horoscopes of devoted couples. When something negative shows in the husband's chart that was not confirmed by his wife's, I am never too disturbed. But when a difficulty in Ronnie's chart was confirmed by what I saw in Nancy's, it was a red alert and time to be extra careful.

I have studied all the most remarkable political horoscopes of the 19th and 20th centuries and the charts of many of the great leaders of the American, European and mid-Eastern historical past. I realized the moment I calculated Nancy's horoscope she was destined to be world famous, and after I succeeded in rectifying Ronnie's, I was certain that these two people had incredible horoscopes, that together they were absolutely fated for world recognition and enormous power.

In our conversations, Nancy and I always called Ronald Reagan "Ronnie." We continued to do this after he became President and it was only on rare occasions that I referred to him as "The President."

## The Presidential Election of 1976

I first met Nancy Reagan in person in the summer of 1976 in San Francisco. A mutual friend of ours invited me to a fund raiser she was organizing for the Reagan campaign. The event took place on a boat on San Francisco Bay.

Nancy gave an anti-abortion speech after the luncheon. I remember her saying, "If you are even considering having an abortion, just pretend there is a window in your tummy and you can see the adorable little baby inside." It was saccharine and cutesy, but I guess it was the sort of speeches she was giving then.

After the speech, everyone flocked to meet her. She said she was particularly interested in meeting me because, while I had done her and the Governor's horoscopes since 1973 and she had watched me on the "Merv Griffin Show" often, she had never actually met me in person. At that time, a great many of my clients came to consult with me in person, so I was also interested in meeting her. Besides, I was helping out with the campaign.

In the early stages of the '76 campaign, a lot of people were

convinced that Reagan would win the nomination instead of
Ford. A William Safire column of June 10th couldn't have
agreed with them more.

> Chicago—The clearest indication that Gerald Ford is going
> to lose the nomination to Ronald Reagan came at the
> conclusion of one of the President's television spots in
> California.
> "Governor Reagan couldn't start a war," the Ford com-
> mercials said. "President Reagan could."
> . . . For those reasons (which liberals are certain to label
> a "death wish") the un-Presidential attack by the President
> will probably deliver the nomination to Governor Reagan.
> Then it will be Reagan vs. Carter—and the Californian's
> turn to move up in the polls, as Mr. Carter does his
> ambiguous best to stay tall in the saddle.

I never for one minute believed that Reagan would win the
Republican nomination in '76. I only helped out as a courtesy to
Nancy. I knew Ronnie would lose. He had the kind of adverse
configuration of Saturn to his horoscope that always causes
political leaders to suffer a defeat. Fortunately, that Saturn
aspect only comes once in 28 years.

I'm not sure what I actually did for the campaign that year. It
wasn't much, or I would remember. And despite what I saw
astrologically, I was hoping that Ronnie would win. I knew from
both Reagans' horoscopes they eventually would land on top.

In mid-September of 1976, the "Merv Griffin Show" asked
me to predict the outcome of the presidential election. I had lost
interest after Reagan failed to win the nomination. I remember I
didn't want to take the time to do the elaborate analysis necessary to be sure of the outcome of the election. But one aspect in
Ford's horoscope stood out in bold relief. The prediction I made
was that in October, Ford would misspeak himself so badly that

it would seriously jeopardize his chances of winning what would be a very close election.

### FORD DENIES MOSCOW
### DOMINATES EAST EUROPE;
### CARTER REBUTS HIM

President Ford said last night in his debate with Jimmy Carter that there was "no Soviet domination of Eastern Europe and there never will be under a Ford Administration."

His statement, which seemed to ignore the long-standing Soviet control of most countries in Eastern Europe, specifically said that Yugoslavia, Rumania and Poland were "independent and autonomous."

His contention that there was no Soviet domination of Eastern Europe brought an instant response by Mr. Carter. "I would like to see Mr. Ford convince the Polish-Americans and the Czech-Americans and the Hungarian-Americans in this country that those countries don't live under the domination and supervision of the Soviet Union behind the Iron Curtain."

—*The New York Times*, October 7, 1976, Front Page

This misstatement, made October 6th, was to haunt Ford during the rest of the campaign. The Carter campaign mentioned it over and over to make sure the voters would not forget. When Ford made his famous remark about the people behind the Iron Curtain, I was struck by the idea that an astrological warning and the choice of a more favorable time to hold the debate might have made the difference in a contest that close.

As an astrologer, one is aware that some events are absolutely fated. Others are not. In the non-fated events, a skillful astrologer can alert people to dangers that can be avoided. The help an astrologer provides can make a promising situation even better. Used intelligently and constructively, astrology can be of the greatest benefit.

It occurred to me at that time that astrology could be used to control the movements and exposure of a politician so as greatly to improve his chances and enable him to avoid any number of pitfalls and dangers. Of course, at that time, I didn't fully realize the extent to which this could be helpful nor had I developed the sophisticated techniques I would later use when I was doing President Reagan's astrology.

# IV

# Ronald Reagan's Horoscope

Even as I now write, Ronald Reagan has had more than his share of criticism, despite his continued popularity with the American public. This is so often the case when, at the end of any great period of history, people too close to the event view it myopically, confusing detail with substance and not having the proper perspective to make the kind of judgment history will make after a hundred years. History itself is not always equal-handed, as in the case of King Richard III when he was unfairly maligned and misjudged. Historians are, after all, only human. They have their particular biases. And like those engaged in other intellectual endeavors including astrology, using the same points of reference, historians disagree. Still, fairly or unfairly, to come to any consensus about how a particular great man will be regarded takes history a very long time.

49

This is how I analyzed my carefully rectified horoscope of Ronald Reagan around the time I decided to submit my written report to the campaign directors in 1980, warning of various avoidable dangers between August 1 and election day.

The Sun in an individual's horoscope is always of prime importance, especially in the case of a president, because it indicates his authority and his dignity. Reagan's Sun is in the sign of Aquarius. There have been five Aquarian presidents, the most famous being Lincoln, F.D.R. and Reagan. These three shared the humanitarian vision so typical of Aquarius, each in his own way. All three were formidable communicators. Lincoln's Gettysburg Address is a masterpiece. Roosevelt's fireside chats brought our nation through a terrible depression which might otherwise have resulted in tragedy. Reagan, a master communicator, turned around the triple economic disasters of double-digit inflation, high interest rates and high unemployment in the space of four years.

Why were all three of these outstanding presidents Aquarians? Was it happenstance or can astrology explain why it happened? The reason is very simple. In the July 4, 1776, birth chart of the U.S.A., the chart with Gemini rising, the Moon is in Aquarius in the part of the chart that has to do with the president.

The Moon in a nation's chart describes the public. It also describes the nation's image of itself, a sort of collective imagining. Reagan's Aquarius Sun on the U.S. Moon indicates a sort of love affair compatibility between the president and the people. It shows that they would see eye to eye.

When the Sun in one chart is on the Moon in another, the two people tend to be soul mates. The Sun person dominates the relationship, while the Moon person sympathizes with the other's way of thinking. The Moon person responds enthusiastically to the ideas, viewpoints and persona of the person represented by the Sun.

In the case of the three presidents, the vast majority of the American public responded naturally to their leadership, although during his lifetime, Lincoln did not enjoy the adulation the other two received.

The Aquarian is a very well-balanced individual. He is first and foremost a humanitarian. While the Aquarian holds himself aloof from the herd (to lead, this is necessary), he is democratic in his attitude toward others. Quite typically, he has friends and admirers in every walk of life. He believes in equality and brotherhood.

While he is idealistic, quite typically he pays more attention to practical matters after he takes over. He is aware that people must have the necessities before their souls can be saved effectively. Thus, Roosevelt paid attention to feeding the hungry during the Depression. And Reagan's first priority after becoming president was to restore the country's troubled economy.

In the 1984 campaign, he could point with justifiable pride to his having turned the economy around after four years in office. Later he was blamed unfairly for the spiraling national debt, a debt that resulted from the runaway spending of his predecessors, beginning after World War II. Congress itself, of course, has the final responsibility for appropriating funds. The national debt is, therefore, the responsibility of Congress. At any rate, Reagan's first priority was to turn around an ailing economy, as he had done after he became governor of California.

Another character trait that has been emphasized in an attempt to make Reagan appear ridiculous is his occasional inattention. Aquarians, quite typically, are bored with uninteresting details, even to the extent of dozing off during a cabinet meeting. This seeming defect can be a very big plus when seen in perspective. The Aquarian leader delegates authority, leaving the details and the modus operandi to others. He pays attention to matters of policy that should rightfully concern him.

This is especially true when, as in Reagan's case, there is no Virgo in the rest of the horoscope. Reagan's horoscope contrasts sharply with Jimmy Carter's. Because of an afflicted Virgo planet in his chart, Carter tried to do everything himself and got lost in details which, as the top executive, he never should have attempted to cope with in the first place.

Aquarian Reagan listened to his advisers and made the important and brilliant decisions, based on what he himself believed. And I will explain further on why circumstance, ill health and those surrounding him made it difficult for him to prevail after the debilitating and depressing personal ordeal of Irangate.

Almost equal in importance to the Sun in an astrological chart is the individual's Moon. Reagan's Moon sign is Taurus. Its position in relation to his Sun indicates that he would divorce. In Taurus, the Moon expresses herself ideally. A Taurus Moon, while essentially conservative, is genial, sound and stable. It is in the portion of his horoscope that couldn't be better for political popularity. It indicates why his conservative ideas and viewpoint have been so widely accepted by the public. His image is that of a conservative primarily, and he is popular because of it, not despite it.

The Moon in a politician's chart describes his image. Reagan is accepted by the public because he is sincere and he states his views positively. His avowed conservatism may seem to conflict with his visionary espousal of SDI, which doesn't seem conservative at all to some people. In many people's view, it is so far out it has been nicknamed "Star Wars." But that is a function of his visionary Aquarian Sun. The most important contribution the Aquarian leader makes is *vision*. He has a vision of what will happen in the future, far in advance of his fellows. While circumstance may make him appear mistaken in the short term, what he sees eventually will come to pass, although he himself may not live to see it. His principles are soundly based on bedrock!

Both the Aquarian and the Taurus elements are in this chart, and each will express itself as his life unfolds. The Moon also represents Nancy—the woman who means most to him in his life—and also his mother.

The third most important part of Reagan's horoscope is his Sagittarius rising sign. Sagittarius is ordinarily the longest lived and luckiest of the signs. Often it indicates a love of horses, sports and outdoor life. His very vitality comes from breathing in fresh air daily. It describes a person whose tastes and behavior are naturally aristocratic, no matter how humble his origins may have been. It describes someone who likes to live rich and is accepted among important affluent people, someone who, himself, manages to attract the good things of life. Also he is religious, and, barring that, very philosophical. Discussion interests him. He likes to exchange ideas and argue back and forth in a civilized fashion. He usually is able to convince the other party to the dialogue of his own ideas and viewpoint.

These three, the Sun, Moon and Rising Sign, are very basic. But the most important planet, by far and away, in Reagan's horoscope is his Jupiter.

Jupiter is the luckiest planet, attached as it is to Sagittarius, the most fortunate sign. Ronald Reagan's Jupiter is in Scorpio. Just physically, this shows tremendous vitality and almost superhuman strength. In this case, it is the planet most descriptive of Reagan himself. Scorpio is the sign of sex and procreation, among other things. Jupiter in Scorpio makes a person feel that his sexual powers (ordinarily these are considerable) come from God, and he equates this also with his physical strength. However, Scorpio normally inclines the body to develop tumors.

Generally, this Jupiter describes the incredible natural vitality that allowed Ronald Reagan to recover from the bullet wound he suffered during the attempted assassination, two serious operations for cancer, the incredible demands of occupying the highest office and the rigors of two campaigns for the presidency as well as weathering the debilitating months of Irangate.

The pivotal planet in a great leader's horoscope describes his mission. In our brief conversation after the State dinner I attended in April 1985, the President told me he felt he had a mission and that his strength to carry it out came from God. I couldn't help smiling when he said it. It is practically word for word the description of Jupiter in Scorpio in my book, *Astrology for Adults*. I can remember my teacher saying when we were looking at historical horoscopes, "A great man, a great animal." Because for a man of action to accomplish great goals, ordinarily he must have tremendous physical stamina. There are, of course, exceptions to this. Gandhi, for instance, was a slight little man; his strength was primarily spiritual.

In a leader's horoscope, Mars indicates his forcefulness in action. Reagan's Mars is in the sign of its exaltation, Capricorn, which gives it its very fullest, most desirable and complete expression. It is placed so that there is also the influence of the sign of Aries, where Mars is most at home. This double influence is also a testimony of great physical force and moral strength, and its relationship to his Saturn describes tremendous executive ability, the ability to rally subordinates and put his plans across. In short, it gives him the power to lead and to inspire his followers.

In Reagan's case, Saturn is in the sign of Taurus. This position enables one to plan like a great general. Ulysses Grant had this position of Saturn. When someone complained to Lincoln that Grant drank too much, he replied, "I'd rather have Grant in the state he is in than twenty other generals sober." It was this combination of a Capricorn Mars with this Taurus Saturn that enabled Reagan to plan his great strategy of refurbishing the military at home and establishing missiles in Europe. This grand design enabled him to deal with Gorbachev from a position of power.

Reagan has the almost incredible distinction astrologically of having three planets in the sign of their exaltation (or fullest expression): Moon in Taurus, Mars in Capricorn and Venus in Pisces. Venus in Pisces is the most loveable indication of all. In his chart, it has to do with worldly prestige and is another reason, if not the most important one, for his great personal popularity. It also gives a very sympathetic love nature and combines with his Mars to add to his voter appeal. This Venus makes an ordinary soul the pet of his family. It made Reagan the pet of the nation.

I have explained to you the astrological indications in Reagan's chart that account for his great vision, a vision which allowed him to develop a grand design of domestic and foreign policy that enabled him to be the most powerful man of action at home and abroad during his eight-year tenure. Now I would like to explain why he was called "the great communicator."

Mercury is the planet that enables one to understand ideas, both to formulate them and explain them to others. Reagan's Mercury in Capricorn, in conjunction with his Capricorn Uranus, gives a ready wit and a natural and irrepressible sense of humor. He made so many wonderful spontaneous remarks. He spoke with such charm. These two planets also indicate originality, and their relationship to his Neptune enables him to speak as if he'd kissed the Blarney Stone; in other words, with great finesse and the charm of the Irish. Mercury in Capricorn also gives depth of thought about practical matters and the memory of an elephant when offended. No one ever has a second chance to offend someone with such a Mercury. Uranus in Capricorn not only accounts for Reagan's great natural charisma, it gives an indomitable will, an almost magical inner will, that in his case motivated him from a humble start to become incredibly successful.

While the position of Reagan's Neptune gives a charming twist to his humor and presentation, it also indicates trouble with some members of the press. This opposition noticeably weakened his will during his last two years in office. It occupies the part of the chart that indicates his wife and his chief of staff and other partners in government. No such sign of weakness surfaced in his first term, when these aspects appeared to represent certain members of the press who almost always opposed him. It is said that if you live long enough, you will experience everything in your birth horoscope. For this reason, it was inevitable that Reagan have these experiences.

Neptune also figures in physical paralysis and cancer. In Reagan's case, it may have referred to a paralysis of will brought on by powerful enemies and the inadequacy of his staff in the autumn of his presidency. Certainly it describes scandal at some time in his life, whether or not he did anything to deserve it.

It is not uncommon for a 20th-century politician to have the planet Pluto prominently placed in his chart. Pluto is a planet of the very greatest complexity. It rules special interest groups as well as the media, and when they combine against you, as indicated when Pluto is adverse, you'd better run for cover. All along, Reagan had media opposition, but he also had support from members of the press and an almost worshipful public, with many special interest groups uniting to help him bring many of his plans to fruition.

Pluto occupies the seventh house angle in Reagan's horoscope. The planets in this angle describe an individual's marriage and other partnerships. It also indicates open enemies. Pluto in an angle can turn opportunity on and off like a hot water faucet. The media refusal to allow Reagan to air his views on national TV—during a Congressional battle over aid to the Contras—forcibly turned off his influence at a crucial moment. All the main networks united in calling his views partisan and political, in effect refusing him a hearing. This is a typical example of Pluto turning on or off to tip the scales in a controversy.

This concludes my description of President Reagan's horoscope, his potential when he entered office, the main indications
in his horoscope of birth, along with illustrations from the
presidential years when applicable. Later, you will see how his
horoscope progressed, how he developed and expanded, and
how he coped with malevolent external forces that could not be
prevented from turning against him.

This then was the horoscope for the remarkable man who
started out the presidency with such magnificent potential. It
was a privilege to contribute astrological advice to him through
Nancy. During my seven Reagan years, I came to know the
President's horoscope better than anyone's.

As with every human being, it was his destiny to undergo
certain experiences. Whenever it was possible, astrology enabled him to avoid danger, to appear always at his best during
the "Teflon years," to change his "Evil Empire" attitude and
send him to Geneva with a plan, well prepared for his first
meeting with Mikhail Gorbachev.

In her memoir, Nancy says, "Fate deals the cards." But she
fails to mention the many important ways their astrologer
helped Nancy and Ronald Reagan to play them.

# V

# The 1980 Campaign

In *My Turn*, Nancy mentions in passing that I had volunteered my services to the 1980 campaign. She writes that she resorted to astrology as a crutch that turned into a habit, that as a former Hollywood actress whose mother was an actress, she, like all people brought up in the theatrical tradition, was very superstitious.

Not for one minute would the pragmatic hardheaded realists running the 1980 Republican campaign have humored a superstitious woman to the extent of following an astrologer's advice had there not been concrete evidence that I could produce results. Nancy's Hollywood background had nothing to do with it. However, her intelligent, constructive use of my astrological expertise during the crucial last three months of the campaign contributed in important ways to Ronald Reagan's victory.

I still laugh when I think of a quip made by my sister, who is involved in the financial world. Ruth was referring to the big traders on Wall Street. "They would go to the zoo in their limousines to consult a caged gorilla if they were convinced that he could predict financial futures successfully."

Now it is true that the campaign's directors normally would not have listened to an astrologer on any subject whatsoever, despite my good Republican credentials and educational background. As far as those in charge were concerned, my advice was heeded for what I was able to contribute in the same way as the pollsters or other professionals they used. I produced results no one else was able to. That was what mattered to them.

I did not become involved with the campaign until after the convention. During the pre-convention period, I became very interested in predicting the outcome of the election. Someone my sister knew who was connected with the Bush campaign asked for my opinion and gave me Bush's approximate birthtime. I studied the horoscopes of all the leading candidates and came to the conclusion that Reagan had by far the best chance of winning.

In July, I called Nancy and asked if she would be interested in my analysis of Ronnie's horoscope and a detailed account of what I saw astrologically for him for the period from August 1st until election day. She said she was delighted to hear from me and that she would be grateful if I would send it as soon as possible.

When she received it, she called to thank me. But I don't think the others thought very much about it until Ronnie made the mistake of telling reporters on August 19th that if he were elected President, he would recognize Taiwan instead of the Republic of China. At that time, Ronnie was perceived to be weak in foreign policy. His two terms as governor of California, while impressive in other areas, hadn't included experience in handling international affairs. His statement had been a real gaffe. While campaign directors were holding their heads and figuring out how to make a convincing recovery, someone noticed that in my report I had underlined in red ink my typewritten warning "not to make any foreign policy pronouncements on August 19th."

From then on, the campaign directors were glued to my report. Nancy called practically daily. She relayed my advice to the others, including the President-to-be.

I now had the chance to put into practice the theory I had come up with because of Ford's unguarded remarks about Eastern Europe in the 1976 debate. For the remainder of the '80 campaign, I gave advice about Reagan's exposure to the media and the public. I chose times of departure when the Reagans rented a private plane.

I particularly remember choosing the time their plane left Washington, D.C., for Philadelphia for the debate with John Anderson. Anderson, if you'll remember, was a minority candidate with two percent of the vote. He wasn't a viable contender, but it was an important debate for Ronnie. It gave him a chance to show his mettle, and the interested TV audience was vast.

When Nancy told me they were going to Philadelphia, I immediately set about choosing a safe and advantageous departure time. Let me explain. The time you set out on a journey determines not only its safety but also whether what you wish to accomplish will fail or succeed. As perfect departure times are the exception, especially when the choice is confined to a limited time period, it is the astrologer's duty to warn the client of any hazards along the way. Where there is any question of interference with the client's plan, the client's success or failure will depend on the astrologer's explicit warning of the type of dangers he will encounter.

As I remember, the exact time I chose was during the morning of the debate. What I saw in the trip chart made me very apprehensive. I told Nancy the plane would arrive safely, but after their arrival, there would be some mechanical difficulty that had nothing to do with the plane. I cautioned her to be sure to check the microphone carefully immediately before the debate was about to begin.

Nancy called me the following day to tell me in amazement that the microphone had been tampered with as I had warned her it would be. Someone had turned it down very low. If it hadn't been checked at the time I told them, Ronnie's voice would have sounded weak and therefore old.

The Carter campaign would have liked nothing better than to make an issue of Ronnie's age. So far, his vital and youthful appearance had given them no opening. But he was the oldest contender for the presidency in American history, and a weak voice coming over the microphone would have left interested voters with a negative impression in this first major TV debate.

During those last three months, Nancy was superstitious about "counting chickens." For my part, I thought it was bad psychology to predict a victory, even one I believed would happen. We both agreed it was better that everyone feel the need to try their hardest up to the very last minute. None of us wanted the campaign workers to relax and take the victory for granted before it was announced officially.

## The Carter-Reagan Debate

Ronald Reagan is a super debater. I cannot claim any credit for his winning the Carter debate. However, I was definitely responsible for Carter's losing that crucial contest on October 28th, shortly before the November 4th, 1980, election, for lose it he did.

About a week before the debate, Nancy was very restive. Nothing startling had happened for either candidate, and Nancy's incredibly astute political instincts were telling her that the Reagan campaign was dead in the water and something had to be done. Nancy was convinced that a debate was the only answer, and she in turn convinced everyone close to them that such a contest between the two candidates had to take place. She hoped it would give the Reagan campaign some sort of dramatic shot in the arm. It was dangerously close to the election. There was no time for a recovery if either candidate made an error. It was definitely kill or cure. We all knew it was a big gamble, but Nancy finally persuaded everyone that her gut feelings were sound.

She consulted me about the timing of the event. I had to give my answer in a hurry, but I did give it a great deal of thought before I chose the time of 9:30 P.M., October 28, in Cleveland, Ohio, to begin the hour-and-a-half-long debate. The time and place chosen to begin a debate determine what will happen during the course of the debate as well as its outcome, who will win and who will lose. To do this expertly, the astrologer must take the horoscopes of both debaters into consideration in relation to the starting time. In this case, I concentrated on what I considered the best opportunity, astrologically: that I reinforce the basic weaknesses in Carter's horoscope and by my expert timing insure that he would trip himself up and lose.

My reasoning was unorthodox from an astrological viewpoint. The average astrologer never would have chosen that time. In order to describe the reasoning that went into my choice of the time for the debate, I must give you some astrological background and describe to you what a "grand trine" means in an individual's horoscope.

Classically, a grand trine is considered lucky. A trine, or 120-degree angle, is the luckiest relationship between two planets and describes good fortune that comes to an individual without his having to make an effort, such as inheriting a fortune from a relative he has never met or experiencing some other stroke of good fortune that comes unsought after and often undeserved. Sometimes a trine in a birth chart describes luck through an agreeable or admirable trait of character that inspires others to respond to the individual in a favorable way. It can also mean that a person has a natural ability to do something easily and well. But generally, what a grand trine indicates is something effortless.

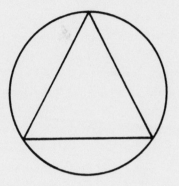

The grand trine is formed by three planets approximately 120 degrees apart. A beginner and some more advanced astrologers might consider this the most fortunate configuration of all. However, I have observed that while a grand trine can be lucky for material good fortune or agreeable characteristics, it can be too much of a good thing. And it tends to make the lucky individual careless or lax.

Some so-called bad aspects can give a person backbone, the need to respond to challenges and the ability to do so. For that reason, they aren't necessarily bad. Squares (90-degree angles), that indicate conflict or adversity or problems, often describe a strong character, someone who works and strives and thus accomplishes a lot. Too much of anything, even good luck, is never unqualifiedly good. As in baseball, a grand trine is like having the bases loaded, so that you can either strike out or hit a grand slam home run.

The Moon, which moves through every sign of the Zodiac in 27½ days, is the fastest moving heavenly body and acts as a catalyst, or agent, in astrology. Typically, it causes two elements in an astrological chart to combine to make things happen. It is rather like the fire that makes two chemicals explode or the baking powder that causes the other ingredients to rise to the top of the cake pan.

At the time of the debate, the moving Moon became the catalyst that activated the grand trine in Jimmy Carter's birth chart. Carter's grand trine was comprised of three planets. His Moon at birth was in Scorpio. (In some cases, this has hedonistic overtones, which may be said to account for Carter's confessed "lusting in his mind.") The other two planets comprising the grand trine were Pluto (the media planet) and Uranus, the planet which gave him a certain charisma. His Uranus was in Pisces, the sign whose symbol is two fish swimming in opposite directions. In its negative manifestations, Pisces can make one rather indecisive.

Carter's Mercury (the planet of speech) in Virgo and his Pisces Uranus (planet of the sudden and unexpected) were opposite one another. Any configuration between Virgo and Pisces can make someone untidy or unable to see the big picture. These people become confused when confronted with too much detail. In Jimmy Carter's case, these two planets gave him every opportunity, astrologically, to speak unguardedly before thinking something over.

After much deliberation, I made up my mind to reinforce the moving Moon with another catalyst: the rising sign. The rising sign of an event is calculated from the minute the event begins. In an individual's chart, the rising sign represents the person himself, his physical body and character type. In a debate chart, it represents the event itself.

The rising sign moves faster even than the Moon does—a degree approximately every four minutes—so that tracking it was the best way to tell what would happen from minute to minute during the course of the debate. I always move the rising sign forward to be able to tell what will happen as the minutes pass and the event unfolds. In the course of the debate, the rising sign placed added emphasis on Carter's grand trine.

In short, I was banking on his getting careless. I knew it was risky. I decided to take a big gamble for the biggest stakes.

Literally on the edge of my chair and figuratively sweating blood and biting my fingernails, I watched the debate on television. I really rooted for Ronnie and in total suspense waited for Carter to fall into my trap.

My analysis turned out to be correct. What I planned to have happen, happened exactly as I had planned. He did what I had anticipated. He became overconfident and careless and did not consider the impression he was making. I had decided on the time that laid a trap.

I don't think that Carter was even aware of how it would strike the viewers when he made his famous remark about consulting his 11-year-old daughter Amy about nuclear energy.

According to *The San Francisco Chronicle*, Carter's awkward moment came when he sought yet another way to drive home his central assertion that nuclear warfare was the key issue of the campaign.

He said, "I had a discussion with my daughter, Amy, before I came here the other day to ask what the most important question was. She said nuclear weaponry." A chuckle ran through the crowd at Carter's source of advice.

The moment he said it, I knew it was all over for Carter. That naïve, ingenuous remark cost him the debate and led to a landslide election in Ronald Reagan's favor on November 4th.

Nancy called me early the morning after the election and described the thrill of driving late at night through Los Angeles streets lined with eager spectators and cheering well-wishers. It was the first of many such experiences for the Reagans. It was the beginning of an incredible adventure. I couldn't have been happier for them. I congratulated Nancy immediately and told her at the end of the conversation to congratulate Ronnie for me.

# VI

# My Working Relationship With Nancy

The question most frequently asked about my professional relationship with Nancy Reagan is how often we talked. This is hard to answer as it varied according to the needs of the moment. However, the basic components of our consultations, the ones that took place regularly, are easy to describe.

The preliminary consultations affecting the President's schedule were routine. Every three months, Nancy would call to tell me what would be needed generally. She would propose certain events and the time frame that was practicable. I would indicate roughly whether certain days were favorable or unfavorable or suitable for some specific activity. Usually, after she told me what was required, I would first tell her what I could see easily. Later, I would get back to her with the exact times that required further study on my part. Of course, these were only very preliminary sessions. As the days progressed, proposals for other activities would come up, and, as it became necessary, Nancy would call until the schedule was completed.

As I've said, I would give Nancy times for all the press conferences or other activities that were more or less routine, and as the President's schedule filled up, she would call for more information. After each session, we would usually arrange a time for her to call back to receive my answers.

Most of the times I supplied were exact to the minute. As President and First Lady, the Reagans were in a position to command the times of most of their appointments. This is one of the great advantages of doing Presidential astrology.

Longer trips demanded much more study on my part. For these, Nancy and I communicated in the beginning of the planning stages: before and during the period when government teams were sent out to make the arrangements, sometimes months in advance, for any extended journey or important event.

Other routine consultations concerned the President's horoscope, which I analyzed on an hour by hour basis. These were some of the most tedious but essential sessions. They took place every two months and lasted at least two hours. I would do one two-hour session for the President, and then the next week I would do Nancy's. These included an overview as well as the very detailed hour-to-hour reports I gave them.

Emergencies were continually coming up, along with the need to fill in busy schedules. When there was a critical emergency or problem to be solved, Nancy would call me sometimes two or three times daily. Except for the bare bones I have just described, the frequency of our consultations varied.

Outside of the report I had submitted to the campaign in

1980, I always refused to write down my advice or predictions. I suggested to Nancy, as I did to all my clients, that she tape my remarks so as to have an accurate record of what I said. But she said she preferred to take it down in writing. She must have had her own version of shorthand because sometimes I was conscious of speaking so rapidly I would be worried that she couldn't keep up with me. Nancy was, however, incredibly well organized, so I suppose she figured out her own way of making the best use of the information I gave her.

At any rate, Nancy would remember everything I told her and mention to me, particularly, when surprising things would happen exactly as I predicted. She would often report back to me, in awestruck tones, an unexpected death or a good surprise, such as an honorary degree, that was reported to her as I had specified during the previous consultation.

## Was Astrology a Habit?

In all fairness, Nancy was in no way addicted to astrology. The need was real. My work was helpful and reliable. I solved problems, gave advice and contributed conceptually. As she could not afford to consult me about frivolous matters, she only called when necessary. We usually exchanged pleasantries at the start of one of the long routine sessions. Then we concentrated at both ends of the phone until we were both exhausted. When it was a matter of problem solving, such as Bitburg or planning the various summits, we would be constantly in touch, often several times a day.

Once in a while, something I suggested didn't make sense according to what Nancy knew from her own viewpoint. In such cases, I would reconsider and supply input that better suited her needs. She was always respectful and polite, and she valued the information and advice I gave her. As I said before, we worked exceedingly well together.

In a successful astrologer-client relationship, it is essential that the client articulate his needs. Nancy was always very explicit and succinct. I never digressed from the subject of interest. In short, we were both far too busy to waste each other's time.

Also it is my policy never to take on a client whose horoscope doesn't show that he or she would benefit by using astrology, or whose horoscope indicates he or she would become overly dependent. I also require that my clients' charts be harmoniously related to my own horoscope.

The frequency with which Nancy consulted me is not nearly as important as the quality and many levels of advice and counseling she received, from the most practical to the most inspirational.

When dealing with more or less routine matters, Nancy would call me on weekends from Camp David. Often, she would call during the week as the need arose.

### The Liaisons

At first, Mary Jane Wick, wife of Charles Z. Wick, U.S. Information Agency Director, served as a liaison between Nancy and me when I needed to get back to her at a time not scheduled at the end of our most recent meeting. Later, my liaison was Betsy Bloomingdale. Once in a while, I called Elaine Crispin, Nancy's social secretary, at the White House. Later, I will detail what happened when other arrangements became necessary.

## How I Was Paid

According to our original agreement, I was paid by the hour both for the time I spent during our phone conversations and the time I spent preparing. In 1985, when I raised my other clients' hourly fees, I didn't raise Nancy's. Later, I was so involved in "Summitry," my only thought was to do quality work. In the last year, I charged Nancy a monthly fixed fee, because she needed much more of my time than she could afford. This was very generous on my part, because I often worked longer than full time. For a while, when an emergency would arise, I was working as long as nine hours uninterrupted.

## Working With Computers

I could not have done this amount of work without the aid of computers. The help they provided was indispensable. I needed hundreds of charts. I would not have been able to calculate so many charts by hand and still have had time left over to analyze them.

Shortly before I began working for the Reagans, I took about a year to get used to having horoscopes and other charts calculated by computer. At first, it was difficult for me, as I used to digest the contents of a chart as I noted each separate element by hand. I soon learned to look at the finished chart and take in at a glance all the elements I had previously absorbed gradually.

What I was able to do with the aid of computerized charts was straight interpretation. This requires continual concentration without letup. I no longer had rote mathematical distractions or the relaxation routine calculating provided. Because of computers, I was able to put into use sophisticated methods of my own invention. that otherwise I would not have had the time or strength to calculate. Not only did computers save tedious hours of work, but without them, the amount of in-depth work I did would have been impossible.

## Who Carried Out My Instructions Concerning the President's Schedule?

In the beginning, Nancy would relay the information I gave her to Mike Deaver, who was very good about seeing to it that what I wanted was done. Later, she relayed my instructions concerning the President's schedule to Donald Regan, who, while he cooperated, resented what Mike Deaver had always expedited routinely without question. Howard Baker had no problem with astrology, and I was never told that he objected to anything Nancy and I had planned.

## Help for Nancy's Personal Problems

Once in a great blue moon, Nancy and I would discuss her personal or family situation, but this was the exception. Mostly we stuck to matters concerned with her role as First Lady and problems that concerned the President or scheduling, according to what I saw astrologically.

Nancy went through certain difficult periods that were un-avoidable. Everybody has them. It comforted her that I could see them in advance and warn her, at the same time advising her on the best way to live through them. The fact that I could predict what would happen to her and to the President meant to Nancy that they were both destined to have certain experiences.

Astrology is a marvelous vehicle for wise action and deep understanding. I do not see how any astrologer could be an atheist or agnostic. I believe that God intends certain experiences for each of us. Astrology is God's way of letting us read His overall plan for our lives.

Astrology operates on many levels: physical, emotional, mental and philosophical or spiritual. The Reagans took complete advantage of all these forms of assistance and advice.

## The President Knew

Nancy was, of course, as I have previously mentioned, the most direct line possible to the President. He had to have known about me and the advice I was giving Nancy. He must have been aware and acquiesced when I gave instructions concerning the timing for certain congressional arm-twisting. When I went through the receiving line at the State Dinner for the President of Algeria, Ronnie leaned down, kissed me and said, "Hello, Joan." After I briefed Nancy for Geneva, his "Evil Empire" attitude toward the Soviet Union changed with no other explanation.

On January 28, 1986, at 11:39:17 A.M., when the space shuttle *Challenger* exploded in mid-launch from Cape Canaveral, killing all seven members of the crew, Nancy called me. She told me the President was trying to decide whether or not to have a complete investigation. He wanted to know what I thought. She asked me to look at the charts of both the takeoff and the explosion.

I analyzed the two charts thoroughly and said that there ought to be an investigation. The Twelfth House indications suggested at worst sabotage, at least inexcusable negligence or some other form of carelessness. It turned out to be true that the Shuttle Program had major flaws. Rocket seal erosion and rocket joint safety had been neglected and the errors were concealed by NASA from the Program Chief.

The work of the Rogers Commission, completed in less than four months, unequivocally identified the cause of the accident, pointed out weaknesses in NASA procedures, and laid a basis for the safer and more successful space program that is a fitting memorial to the *Challenger* crew.

The President had asked Nancy to ask me about going to Reykjavik; he and Shultz followed my advice to negotiate there as long and as hard as possible, and following my advice they stayed later than planned. Ronnie asked Nancy, "What does Joan say?" when he wanted to know when the Irangate ordeal would be over. And he phoned to thank me personally for a letter written at the end of Irangate, in which I described myself as his astrologer, addressing him as "Dear Ronnie" and signing it "Joan."

There is no doubt whatsoever in my mind that the President was fully aware of the contribution I made: the scheduling, my ideas, the problems I solved and the advice I gave.

# VII

# Astrology Was the Teflon in the "Teflon Presidency"

Washington still talks about Ronald Reagan's "Teflon" presidency, usually discussed with irritated admiration à la ABC's Sam Donaldson. The Teflon presidency means that no matter what gaffes (as defined by the media) President Reagan commits, no blame seems to attach to him; that is, no mud sticks, no smears seem to affect his popularity.
—Arnold Beichman, *Wall Street Journal*, Nov. 2, 1984

For the better part of six years, my advice to both Reagans guided Nancy to achieve for a time an enviable image and immunized the President from the hazards of office that from time to time ordinarily afflict the reputations of political men. In short, astrology assured that nothing unfavorable would "stick" to the President. They said it was like teflon. Let me describe how I was the Teflon in what came to be known for the better part of six years as the "Teflon Presidency."

## The Press Conferences

As he was for the rest of the team that backed him up, President Reagan was an ideal subject for an astrologer. His natural charm and personal charisma, as well as his authoritative manner, were qualities Americans admired and loved.

For almost six years, the President dominated his press conferences, partially because he was well prepared and knew his answers, partially because he had the ability to think on his feet, and finally because the times I chose for his press conferences enabled him to appear at his best.

Everyone, even the smoothest, silver-tongued orator, has off moments. I doubt that anyone exists who has not said something that didn't come out the way he intended it to sound. The average president, exposed constantly to the public, is particularly vulnerable to this mishap. While most people have unguarded moments, a slip of the tongue is particularly held against public men. Until I took over the task of guarding President Reagan's tongue by astrology, he had a tendency to come out not infrequently with real bloopers and other remarks better left unsaid.

For the seven years I served the administration, I always chose the times for presidential press conferences. The best times for the first ones turned out to be eight o'clock in Washington, i.e., five o'clock on the West Coast. Most of the press conferences followed the eight o'clock pattern. The rare exceptions when the eight o'clock time was unfavorable were held at nine o'clock Eastern Standard Time.

Ordinarily, the time an astrologer chooses to begin a debate or press conference determines the hazards along the way, as well as its reception by the public and the media.

I was always particular that this beginning chart be favorable. Then I would move the original chart forward minute by minute to see when the President would be particularly well showcased and when the detractors needed to be squelched. I would tell Nancy which portions of the half-hour sessions were hazardous, so that the President could be careful. And if the beginning time was not as propitious for questioning, he could lengthen his opening remarks.

I always tried to have the portion of the chart representing the President well fortified and favorably configurated by the planets. I tried, insofar as possible, to have the portion ruling journalists and the rest of the media either in agreement with the President's indicators or arranged so that he would come out on top. His prestige and publicity indicators also had to be excellent.

In the beginning, when most of the current movements of the planets were in favorable relationship to the President's horoscope, it was fairly easy to find suitable days for press conferences. They were held frequently, but always at a time that promised a favorable result. I treated them as I treated debate charts. I saw to it that he would show off to best advantage. I showcased the President by choosing optimum times for him to make an appearance.

My operating principles were classic in the beginning, yet I followed each conference avidly, moment to moment, glancing from my charts to the television, which flashed the President's image as well as the time. The more press conferences I did, the more I refined my techniques and improved on them. I also had ways of insuring that even if the President did make a slight error when speaking, it wouldn't be held against him and would be forgotten or glossed over rapidly. During the "Teflon" period, by my guidance, he was insured that the few minor errors he made didn't "stick" to him.

## The Speeches

I chose the times for President Reagan's speeches, with the exception of a few emergencies when necessity dictated that the speech begin at a particular time. The speech following Reagan's return from Reykjavik was one of these exceptions.

Speech times were easier than press conferences because only three factors were involved: the reaction of the American people and of the media, and the President's getting his point across. Ronald Reagan wasn't called "the great communicator" for no reason. No one, not even Franklin Delano Roosevelt, delivered speeches better than he. My role, like that of the speech writers, made something that was already magnificent even better.

## Public Appearances

Choosing the times for public appearances, like speeches and press conferences, was fairly routine. Every few months, when Nancy knew where Ronnie needed to make appearances or attend a fund-raising function or give a non-televised speech, we would get together by telephone and plan. I would often rule out times that had tentatively been chosen because of the safety factor or because the general configurations of the planets were adverse or because of planetary movements counter to the President's chart.

### Detailed Daily Predictions for the President

I have a very complicated astrological technique which enables me to predict what is happening to an individual from moment to moment. I have discussed my method with several astrologers who have said that nothing would persuade them to do for anyone something so tedious and time consuming.

I did it for the President, and to a lesser extent for Nancy. I particularly remember that in our last consultation about the President's horoscope, I kept seeing frequent references to his astrologer in May 1988. I remember telling Nancy, "Ronnie's astrologer will handle some difficult situation well and protect him." It puzzled me when I predicted it, and only after the Donald Regan book was published did I realize specifically what it would mean.

It has been reported that I told the Reagans whether they would have good days or bad days or whether something should take place in the morning or afternoon. I only wish it had been that simple. It wasn't. After I had chosen a good day or eliminated a bad one, the timing of the actual event would be precise, to the minute.

### Bringing Two People into Agreement

An expert astrologer can sometimes bring two people into agreement rather easily if the time period offers an opportunity to do this sort of thing.

Nancy would sometimes ask me to help out when a bit of arm-twisting was needed. For instance, if a member of Congress occupied a pivotal position and could swing a vote or add his vote or persuade others to pass a bill the President wanted, I was called upon. I was never told who the person was who

As with most of my other clients, my consultations with Nancy Reagan usually took place over the telephone, as I read from the chart, giving advice and predictions. Some of our sessions lasted for several hours, and Nancy took notes as I spoke to her. (Russ Fischella)

# Astrological Chart for
# Ronald Reagan's Oath of Office

### January 20, 1985 · 11:56:50 AM · EST · Washington, DC

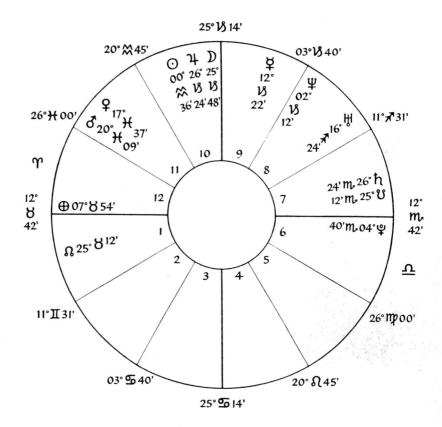

The Inaugural Oath must be taken by the President of the United States on January 20th of the year following the November election. For President Reagan's swearing-in for his second term, I was also forced by circumstance to choose a moment fairly near noon. (Nicki Michaels)

Given the midday requirement for President Reagan's second swearing-in, I could not eliminate a certain unfavorable relationship between planets which showed danger to the President, the possibility of assassination or scandal of some sort, and espionage. The chart also showed a breakthrough in foreign policy, and an agreement with a major foreign power. Above, Chief Justice Warren Burger gives President Reagan the oath of office in the Rotunda of the Capitol as Nancy holds the Bible. (AP/Wide World Photos)

In April of 1981, Nancy asked me to advise her about reshaping her image; at the time she was heavily criticized for everything from the White House china she planned to buy to her expensive clothes. Left, she is seen attending a Gala Dinner in Madrid, and below, she and the President leave the White House in January 1981 en route to a round of inaugural balls.

**S AND YOUTH:**

**National Federation Parents for Drug-Free Youth**

**ₗICAN S**

DRUGS AND YOUTH:

National Federation c Parents for Drug-Free Youth

AN AMERICAN CRISIS

(UPI/Bettmann Newsphotos)

Left, the "new" Nancy addresses a conference for the National Federation of Parents for Drug-Free Youth, and below, she visits two Korean children who were in the U.S. for heart surgery.

(AP/Wide World Photos)

In 1980, John Anderson was a minority candidate, but the debate with him was still important to Reagan. Because of what I saw in the chart of the debate, I told Nancy to check the microphone carefully. Amazingly, Nancy called the following day and told me that the microphone had indeed been tampered with, and had she not checked it, Ronnie's voice would have sounded weak and therefore old. (UPI/Bettmann Newsphotos)

I chose 9:30 P.M. on October 28, 1980, for the beginning of Reagan's debate with Carter. The planetary configuration at that time showed that Carter might speak unguardedly. My analysis turned out to be correct. When Carter made his now famous remark about consulting his eleven-year-old daughter, Amy, about nuclear energy, it was all over for him. Reagan won the election in a landslide victory.

(UPI/Bettmann Newsphotos)

Nancy asked me to select the times and places for the two Reagan-Mondale debates in 1984. I really goofed in my choice for the first debate. It was the only time I failed the Reagans or gave them less than excellent advice. My choice for that debate, instead of emphasizing Mondale's lack of charisma (as I had intended), livened him up and gave him pizzazz. My choice for the second debate, however, insured that Ronnie would emerge victorious.

My control over the departure times of Air Force One when the President was aboard was absolute. The safety for an entire trip can be seen in the chart cast up for the departure time, so it is of the utmost importance. (UPI/Bettmann Newsphotos)

Nancy asked me to pick a favorable time for the announcement of Anthony Kennedy's Supreme Court nomination. The time I chose was 11:32:25 A.M. on November 11, 1987. The announcement was done with great care and precision; a man with a stopwatch gave the signal for the President to make the announcement. Below, as President Reagan looks on, Kennedy gives the thumbs up after taking the constitutional oath and becoming the 104th Supreme Court justice in United States history. (AP/Wide World Photos)

needed persuading, but Nancy would report back to me that it worked out reliably.

I particularly remember one occasion when I picked my time, but it turned out to be twenty minutes after 1:00 P.M. I suggested that the President invite the Congressman for a one o'clock luncheon. I told Nancy to tell him to make pleasantries and tell jokes or whatever, but to stall until 1:20 and then to suggest what it was he wanted to accomplish. The President had to know it was because of me that he had to wait twenty minutes before broaching the subject. Otherwise, waiting wouldn't have made sense.

This is an example of what I did when political arm-twisting was necessary. It always worked out during the "Teflon" years. During Irangate and even during the later attempts to help out the Contras in Nicaragua, the major cosmic forces had so turned against Reagan that what I had been able to do earlier was impossible for me to do then.

## Short Trips

A typical short trip, when the President would start out in the morning and return by late afternoon, was treated astrologically like any other matter. First, a favorable day was selected, then a time of day for the departure that would assure a safe return, the success of the venture and good publicity.

Often short trips were taken on less than perfect days. I could use them before the indicators turned negative, because the President would already have left and returned. However, on long journeys, this was a different matter. The important indicators had to be perfect and a choice of time involved a great deal more work.

## The State of the Union Speeches

Unlike the Inauguration chart that had to be done on the twentieth of January, I had some leeway with the State of the Union addresses. These could take place at the end of every January within the space of a few days. Like important journeys or other important speeches, they had to be done at a vintage time. Fortunately, even at the worst of times, I was able to chart these successfully.

## All Public Appearances of Any Importance

Reagan had configurations in his horoscope very much like Lincoln's in several respects, all very important and one of which I will describe in a later chapter. The first way in which their charts were similar was in the the danger of assassination in theaters or other places of amusement, and I was always on pins and needles whenever such appearances were mandatory. I told Nancy she could not be too careful of security during Ronnie's annual December attendance at a Washington, D.C., Christmas performance in the Kennedy Center theater and always to have a red alert to the secret service every year as a matter of course. Because he absolutely had to go to these performances, I used to check his special indicators with extra care. Sometimes it was a little iffy. Had it been actively dangerous, I think I would have been forceful about warning Nancy and persuading them not to go. Luckily, this never came at a time when his birth chart configuration was fatalistically and unavoidably brought out.

Lincoln's death was absolutely fated. The part of his horoscope that represented his physical body that night in the Ford theatre came together with the part of his birth horoscope that represented death, at the moment he was shot. There was no way even the finest astrologer could have prevented Lincoln's assassination.

However, while Reagan had times when he could have been assassinated, I was always able to protect him. These times had mostly to do with current external movements of the planets in relation to his birth chart or the progressions (current positions of the planets) within his horoscope, and while they indicated considerable danger, they could all be avoided by my warning him not to appear in public at vulnerable times.

Astrology, like all of life, is a rather fascinating combination of fate and free will. Philosophers have argued for centuries which takes precedence. I think at different times one or the other predominates. The "free will" times are when the astrologer can be helpful. He can alert his client to avoid an avoidable danger. But sometimes, as in the case of Lincoln's death, it is absolute fate and there is nothing an astrologer could do.

In Reagan's case, these "free will" times when I alerted him helped him avoid preventable accidents. This was not easy for me. I will describe how I went about it in the section about the President's safety in a general sense.

The danger factor is ever present in connection with any president. In the case of a zero-year president and one with the vulnerability I've just described in his birth horoscope, the assassination danger was an ever-present worry and had to be taken into careful consideration in everything that was planned.

My usual technique for avoiding that danger was never to expose him to the public at vulnerable times any more than I let him risk danger to his reputation by speaking when he would be likely to make a blunder. Aside from this, I treated public appearances like every other time I chose for the President, insuring that they would end in success.

At the end of 1985, Reagan's approval rating, 68 percent, was not as high as it had been, but it was higher than any of the recent two-term presidents at the beginning of the second term.

For the better part of six years, I was able to serve as the "Teflon," until the cosmic forces turned against Reagan with such virulence and for so long a period that the "Teflon" years came to an end.

## The President's Safety

I have already described how I guarded the President's safety routinely, monitoring his exposure to the public within the United States. During all public appearances, including press conferences and short trips within the country, I stood guard astrologically. However, planning trips abroad by astrology was more difficult, time consuming and complex.

My control over the departure times of Air Force One when the President was aboard was absolute. This was a matter of safety, first and foremost, both at home and abroad. I always gave these times the most careful consideration. Safety is to be seen in the chart calculated for the departure time. I was always extra careful to scrutinize in every particular this kind of chart.

Doing presidential astrology has great advantages from an astrologer's standpoint. To be able to order a plane to depart at twenty minutes after the hour instead of on the hour or half hour is a great advantage. The astrologer can be sure her plans will be carried out exactly.

In the beginning, I'll have to admit I didn't think too much about my role. I was accustomed to determining flight times for clients who had private planes. It is hard for an astrologer to cope with the uncertain schedules and delayed takeoffs of commercial aircraft.

One day, after I had changed the time Ronnie was originally scheduled to leave Washington, Nancy said, "Joan, do you realize that you are ordering the time for the takeoff of Air Force One?" She told me she'd call Andrews Air Force Base

immediately. I remember being somewhat startled by her remark. It was the first time I'd thought about it as anything
unusual. It really brought home to me the enormity of what I'd
been doing routinely. The responsibility of what I'd undertaken
suddenly loomed large.

Bill Plante of CBS said that White House correspondents
often wondered about the unusual departure times for Air
Force One. He commented that it would often be twenty
minutes past or before the hour. "We wondered if there was any
strategy involved and were relieved to learn that the obvious
reason was astrology."

The original departure time is the most important factor for
general safety on a trip. But I never took chances. I cast a chart
for both Reagans for the various locations during the time they
would be away. In addition, I cast the charts for the countries
and cities, when available, for the time of the Reagans' visits, as
well as the mundane material for the proposed location, which
included the Solar Ingresses, Lunar cycles and cycle charts of
the planets Mars, Jupiter, Saturn, Uranus and Neptune. The
Pluto cycle is too problematical and inexact. I also cast the charts
for takeoff times during an extended journey, as well as the
times of the landings, to have a better idea of what to expect at
every stop. It goes without saying that I was extra careful to
study what was going on in the Reagans' personal charts during
trips.

I only allowed Ronald Reagan to go any place, including
outside of the White House, at safe times. The general advice I
gave Nancy covered Washington, but when a trip was scheduled, especially a long one, I had to cast up some of the charts
by hand. Nicki Michaels, who does my computer work, would
have caught on had I ordered a chart for Santa Barbara, for
instance, after ordering a chart for Washington. A place like
Reykjavik, Iceland, ordered in advance of the summit's announcement in the media, would have been a dead giveaway. I

would sometimes use a large computer service for some of the charts. By dividing up the work between Nicki and Astro-Numeric Service, I saved myself a certain amount of busy work.

But I did everything possible to preserve absolute secrecy. You can imagine the terrible danger to the President were an assassin to learn of the highly sensitive information I had to be given in order to help Nancy determine the President's whereabouts at all times.

## The President's Health

In July of 1985, the President's horoscope showed that he would undergo surgery. Ordinarily when I see a health problem in a client's chart, I try to warn him without alarming him. If it shows in the client's chart that the doctors won't discover it in time, I advise the client to have a checkup, indicating the part of the body likely to have trouble. I always caution my clients well in advance and keep insisting on frequent checkups. Later, you will see how I handled Nancy's breast cancer.

President Reagan had a Scorpio ruler, which gives a tendency to tumors, so constant vigilance on the part of his doctors was indicated from an astrological viewpoint. A benign polyp was removed in May 1984. It was Reagan's own doctors who made the decisions not to order either a barium X-ray enema or a colonoscopy or both in March 1985, when the second polyp was found. I had absolutely nothing to do with that. I am not a doctor.

The discovery that the President did, in fact, need an operation came on July 10. The doctors wanted to operate immediately, but I told Nancy that the 13th at noon was a better time for the operation to take place.

I was definitely responsible for the delay between July 10 and July 13 of 1985. It is because of me that the operation was successful and that there was no recurrence of cancer between July 1985 and President Reagan's departure from office. The three-day delay was of no importance medically. Had they operated before the time I chose, they would have risked not removing the cancerous growth completely. The fact that the cancer did not recur is due to the excellent time I chose astrologically. However, as I said, the President has a tendency to develop tumors.

My credentials for planning the time to begin surgery are excellent. Surgeons who have relied on me for doing this type of planning have thanked me. I especially remember one lung cancer operation. After I chose the time, I said there would be unexpected complications but that the operation would be successful. When the surgeon cut the patient open, he found a tumor double the size he had anticipated from the X-ray. The operation took much longer than expected. Afterwards, the surgeon looked as if he had aged ten years. He told me he got through the unexpected difficulties almost miraculously. He said he couldn't have gone through it without my help. He was a first-rate surgeon, and he didn't scoff at using astrology.

For centuries, astrology and medicine went hand in hand. The famous astrologer Evangeline Adams learned astrology from Dr. Heber J. Smith, a Boston physician who always consulted the patient's horoscope before examining him.

A Florida ear, eye, and throat physician, Dr. Edson J. Andrews, made a study of several thousand patients and came to the conclusion that bleeding was worse at the time of a full moon. He proved by scientific study something astrologers have taken for granted for centuries.

At any rate, around the time of the July 13 operation, the President's sensitive indicator showed not only surgery but other difficulties. I believe Robert McFarlane insisted on seeing the President in the hospital. While I didn't know about it at the time, what he told the President contributed to the Irangate scandal which even as I write is under investigation.

### Charts of Trips for Success and Safety:
### The Philippines and the Far East in November of 1983

An example of the type of long, complex trip abroad I worked
on astrologically for the President was his journey to the Philippines, Japan and South Korea in early November of 1983. It was
a major project and included many stops, side-trips and appearances, all of which I timed very carefully. It was particularly
frightening because of the fatal shooting of the Philippine opposition leader, Benigno Aquino, Jr., in August and the bombing
in Rangoon, Burma, that killed 21 people, including four South
Korean ministers, the previous month. Being conscientious, I
not only did takeoffs and landings but all the many other charts
necessary for such an extended and important trip. It included
stops in Hololulu and Manila. On November 6, Air Force One
left the Philippines at 9:30 A.M. for Tokyo.

## REAGAN MAY EASE NAKASONE'S BLUES

Tokyo—It may not be what he had in mind, but when
President Reagan arrives for a state visit this week, he will
probably find himself caught up in a political campaign.
. . . For Prime Minister Yasuhiro Nakasone, Mr. Reagan's
trip could not have come at a more opportune time.

In Japan, political analysts say voters do not pay much
attention to foreign affairs But Mr. Nakasone has based a
good part of his appeal on his international style, especially
his relations with Mr. Reagan. These have been friendly,
to the point that they call each other "Ron" and "Yasu."
—Clyde Haberman, *The New York Times*, November 5,
1983.

The President's visit to Tokyo was a great success. Despite

the problems of trade relations and the lopsided balance of payments, Nakasone and Reagan always got along famously. Among the side-trips I timed for this journey was President Reagan's visit to Nakasone's old farmhouse retreat 37 miles west of Tokyo where Japanese security was very tight.

When I was first told of the President's intentions to visit troops in the demilitarized zone between North and South Korea, I was concerned (as was Nancy) with Ronnie's safety. We had to be. The President was fearless. His personal safety was less of a concern to him than the safety of the country and its citizens. That was always of prime importance to him.

I finally chose the time of 10:00 A.M. on November 14th for his visit to the troops in the DMZ. At Japan's Imperial Palace, he changed from his pin-striped suit to an olive-drab battle parka. He visited and worshipped with American troops and viewed North Korea through binoculars before making an inspirational speech to the soldiers who regularly stand duty at the DMZ. The time I chose protected the President by insuring that he would be hidden from the enemy, that he would make a lot of young friends and that the visit would be well publicized.

Francis X. Clines of *The New York Times* wrote, "If all the world's a stage, then President Reagan has just played the palace and the troops in the trenches in the same week."

Reagan reaffirmed his pledge to help South Korea militarily during his time in Seoul. Everything on the trip went well and smoothly and Ronald Reagan returned safely to Washington.

## The China Trip

Air Force One arrived in Beijing, China, at 2:00 P.M. on April 25, 1984. The chart showed tremendous prestige for the American President, commanding global attention and a great deal of favorable publicity. It guaranteed diplomatic friendships and elaborate entertainments and ceremonies. As the Moon in that chart is exactly on the degree of Gorbachev's most important planet (although he had not yet assumed the position of Secretary General), this visit of the American President to Beijing was at that time of great concern to Gorbachev. It was an excellent chart that showed the trip was taken in a spirit of adventure, and it guaranteed that the Americans would be enormously well received.

Of course, the arrival chart was only one of the charts I took into consideration. There was the chart for the founding of Communist China as well as the geographical location charts for Beijing. In addition, the President's sensitive indicator had to be checked out for that location at the time. You can see that I took nothing for granted, both for safety and a fortunate visit. It worked out very successfully.

## The Economic Summit in Tokyo

The trip for the Economic Summit in Tokyo took a great deal of planning. For instance, I scheduled the Reagans to leave Washington for Los Angeles on April 25, 1986 at 9:35 A.M. This time was defective because the day during which they traveled was safe, but the chart did not last for the total period of the trip. The time chosen for them to leave Los Angeles, on the other hand, was excellent: 9:10 A.M. on the 26th. I reasoned that it was really the beginning of the trip because they were then leaving the continental United States for the Far East.

At this Economic Summit, the President particularly wanted to make a strong statement against terrorism with economic sanctions against Libya. The Italians backed out, but Margaret Thatcher sided with Reagan.

## The President's Trip to Grenada

The U.S. invasion of the little island of Grenada in November of 1983 was controversial. The media had not been alerted and there was a general outcry because the swift U.S. military action caught everyone by surprise. It was over quickly with minor casualties. French President Valéry Giscard d'Estaing supported President Reagan. He said, "Taking into consideration the Cuban presence on the island of Grenada and also the construction of an airfield whose nature does not correspond to the normal needs of the island, I approve of the American intervention on Grenada."

In early 1986, polls showed growing numbers of Americans wanted the defense budget cut. To remind the country of the grand victory days for U.S. military forces, President Reagan visited Grenada on February 20th. I chose the time of 7:55 A.M. for Air Force One to take off. The Sun that day was very close to the President's Venus, which signifies his popularity and public standing, and the moving Jupiter was not far away. The trip was triumphant with the luckiest planet, Jupiter, on one of the three luckiest planets in Ronald Reagan's chart. There were also very favorable aspects of the Moon.

# VIII

# The 1984 Election Campaign

The only real hitch the campaign team had to deal with during those weeks of planning in the fall of 1983 was a conflict over when the President should formally declare his candidacy. [Lee] Atwater, in particular, wanted it done right away, but he was repeatedly told that Mrs. Reagan did not feel the time for that announcement was "propitious." That baffled him, and when he continued to press for an explanation, [Michael] Deaver finally took him aside and disclosed that Nancy's reluctance was based on an astrologer's warning.

— *The Acting President: Ronald Reagan and the Supporting Players Who Helped Him Create the Illusion That Held America Spellbound* by Bob Schieffer (CBS News Washington Correspondent) and Gary Paul Gates

The Reagans had deliberated for months about his running for a second term. Their children, Ron and Patti, were against it. In the fall of 1983, Nancy told me that she and Ronnie had decided to enter the presidential race. Both he and Nancy wanted to make the announcement in early December.

I did not like the astrological indications for December of 1983. I persuaded the Reagans to wait until the end of January, when I had found a time as near to perfect for entering a contest as any I have seen in all the many years I've practiced astrology. The chart was not only superb in itself, it accorded with the President's horoscope so amazingly that I felt if he declared his intention to run at the time I chose, he was a cinch to win the election.

It was rather an odd time: 10:55 P.M. just before the late night news, Sunday, January 29, 1984. Like every other chart for beginning a venture, it showed not only the events along the way, but the way the project would end. A declaration-to-run-for-office chart based, as are all elective charts, on the time and place of its beginning, tells the astrologer how the matter will turn out. The astrologer treats it exactly as if someone were to enter a contest of any kind.

In this particular chart, the planets were grouped in the part of the chart that referred to the person making the declaration to run. It was sort of like sitting in a poker game and holding a royal flush.

It was obvious to other astrologers that an astrologer had picked the time. I remember a colleague of mine sending me a letter with the chart of the announcement time enclosed. Her friend made this comment. "This time was not only chosen by an astrologer, it was chosen by a master astrologer." I said, "Oh, does she really think so?" There was a comment to the same effect in the *AFA Bulletin* and other astrological magazines. It was common knowledge among those in the astrological community and others that the Reagans used astrology. However, no one knew who the astrologer was. And I wasn't about to say anything.

I only made one important error the entire seven years I did the Reagans' astrology. And that was a really glaring one. However, I think because the declaration-to-run chart was such a good one, my mistake turned out better than if it hadn't been made.

Nancy asked me to select the times and places for the two Reagan-Mondale debates. I chose October 7 in Louisville, Kentucky, for the first one. My fallacious reasoning went as follows. Ordinarily, one would put the Sun of the person selected by the astrologer to be the winner in the most prominent place in the person's location chart.

I selected not only a time and place for the actual debate. I also considered each candidate's location chart. The location chart tells what will happen to a particular person at a given time in a given place. With Mondale in the first debate, I did something rather unusual. I put his Sun in a prominent position in the location chart for the time and place of the debate. I reasoned that he had so little charisma and personality that the Sun, normally indicative of these traits, prominently displayed, would simply emphasize his deficit characteristics.

Instead, the Sun's rays livened him and gave him real pizazz. It taught me something I already knew, but I guess I needed to know it in blood. Wherever the Sun is placed in an individual's chart, he shines forth. And unaccustomed as Walter Mondale was to doing so in the presence of a master debater such as the President, that one afternoon he turned in a spirited performance.

As I said, it was the only time I failed the Reagans or gave them less than excellent advice. The seven years I devoted to being their astrologer, my own horoscope showed that I would do absolutely inspired work. But I have to admit, that time I really goofed.

I must say, Nancy was a lady about it. She never mentioned what had happened or blamed me in any way. She simply said, "They rehearsed Ronnie badly. They crammed him so full of facts and figures, it threw him off." As we never discussed it, I didn't go into the fact that it had been my error. Just as I had succeeded in trapping Jimmy Carter into doing his worst, I had enabled Mondale to show off to advantage during that first debate.

I didn't hear from Nancy for about a week. Then she called. The time for the second debate was imminent. I had chosen the time and place for the second debate, but I had stuck to tried-and-true methods, both in the candidates' charts and the debate chart. I knew that on the 21st of October, in Kansas City, Ronnie would emerge victorious. But I was nervous about what I had done on the first debate.

When Nancy called, she said she had been busy arranging for Ronnie's briefing, that there would be plenty of time for it and that she had seen to it that the people responsible for briefing him wouldn't over-rehearse him. Then she had arranged for an audience and some stirring music to greet him shortly before the debate began, to put him in an optimistic humor.

I don't know who was responsible for Reagan's witty put-down that squelched Mondale forever. During the debate, Henry Trewhitt of the *Baltimore Sun* said that John Kennedy had had to go for days without sleep during the Cuban missile crisis, and then Trewhitt asked the President: "Is there any doubt in your mind that you would be able to function in such circumstances?"

"Not at all," Reagan said, "and I want you to know that I also will not make age an issue in this campaign. I am not going to exploit, for political purposes, my opponent's youth and inexperience." Ronnie's remark was a classic. Nancy said Ronnie thought it up on the spur of the moment. But I think that like everything else connected with that particular crucial second and final debate, it had been planned carefully.

Walter Mondale had shown off to such advantage during the first debate, it was astonishing. It was as out of character for him to give a spirited performance as it was out of character for Ronnie to turn in an average one. What happened wasn't all bad, however. It had the advantage of stimulating more interest in the second debate and a larger television viewing audience than it ordinarily would have drawn. People were glued to their sets to see whether or not this debate would be the same as the first or whether the champion would emerge triumphant. All I could think when it was over was that it was a good thing I had made my mistake on the first debate rather than on the crucial final one.

At the time Mondale chose his running mate, there was a great deal of interest as to which of two women candidates for vice-president he would choose. My mother had said, "It's perfectly obvious."

We were astonished and asked her, "Why?"

She said, "It will be Ferraro. You'll see."

When Mondale announced that Ferraro would be his running mate, we were mystified about why Mother had been so certain.

"It's simple," she said. "Dianne Feinstein [then Mayor of San Francisco] is taller than Mondale. She would have dwarfed him in all their pictures together. Because of the impression on the voters, he had to choose the shorter woman."

It was canny of Mother to think of it. I also think the same thing applied to Bush's choice of Quayle, in a slightly different context. This time it wasn't physical stature. It was Quayle's inexperience and a lack of stature in other ways that made Bush choose a vice-presidential running mate who would play up his own greater strength and who would in no way dominate him. Dukakis was not as clever when he chose Bentsen.

## The Inaugural Chart for the Second Term

The Inaugural Oath must be taken by the President of the United States on January 20th of the year following the November election. There is no way of getting around this and postponing the Inauguration to a more favorable date. It must be done on the 20th.

In this case, I not only had to work within the time limit of a particular day, I also had to choose a moment fairly near noon. The planets were in reasonably good configuration at the time, with one exception. I disposed of the one unfavorable relationship among three planets as best I could. Of course, it was impossible to eliminate it entirely.

It showed danger to the President, the possibility of assassination or scandal of some sort, and also espionage. It was impossible to remove the unfavorable configuration from the chart. Given the mid-day requirement, I couldn't even *minimize it.*

The chart had a great many pluses, however, that more than made up for the negative parts. It showed a fabulous breakthrough in foreign policy that would be remembered always. It showed an agreement with a major foreign power that would result in the President's being remembered forever for having made the rapprochement.

Every planet except for Pluto occupied the top half of the horoscope circle. This promised prominence. It was an extraordinary chart. Jupiter, the most fortuitous planet, occupied the part of the horoscope that referred to the President. Because the Sun was in the humanitarian and visionary sign of Aquarius in the Presidential segment of the chart and the Moon was in the same segment, these two emphasized the importance of the President's role. The planet Mercury was placed in the department of foreign affairs beautifully, in excellent configuration with a number of planets.

It never occured to me when I was choosing this time for the

Inaugural Oath of Office that another interpretation could be added to the one I've just described.

The eighth house of a horoscope means a lot of things in a mundane or political chart. It describes the taxes, the national debt and money owing to other nations, and it also is the house of astrology. Jupiter, the planet connected with this house, is in the mid-heaven (the most prominent place) in the Inaugural chart in second term. This could indicate that astrology would influence the President and would play an important role in relations with foreign powers. Jupiter, the planet of astrology (among other things), in this particular chart shows that the astrologer's advice would not only be benevolent, it would be very fortunate. It even showed that the astrologer would be a woman, because the Moon, or feminine principle, was involved in the configuration.

But as I say, the thought that astrology would be so instrumental in this second term honestly didn't occur to me then. And even had it done so, with the time restrictions imposed on me, I could not have altered it significantly. Evidently it was meant to be.

Both George Bush and Michael Deaver timed the oath of office on which I based this chart. There was approximately four minutes' difference between the times the two of them gave Nancy. I chose Bush's time over Mike Deaver's because, as I used the chart, it seemed to me more accurate. Mike, of course, knew why he was choosing a time. I don't suppose the then Vice-President knew, but he did it better than Deaver.

# IX

# My April 1985 Visit
# to Washington

I didn't go to either of the inaugurals because of the bad weather
and the crowds. But my stars for Washington, D.C., in 1985
during the second week of April were so auspicious that I
decided to pay a visit to Washington then.

When I told Nancy I was coming, she said, "We're having a
State Dinner for the Algerians on Wednesday that week. I'll
send you an invitation immediately. This time," she promised,
"there won't be a slip-up. O.K.?"

What Nancy was referring to was the State Department
dinner for Queen Elizabeth II that took place in San Francisco
in March 1983. That time I had not received an invitation. After
the dinner took place, Nancy had called and said she missed
seeing me in the receiving line.

"There must have been some mistake." She had been very apologetic. "I know I put your name on the list."

This time, I received an invitation both to the State Dinner for the Algerians and the welcoming ceremonies the morning of the day before.

Nancy also invited me to tea in her private apartments the day after the dinner. She offered to arrange for me to have a tour of the White House.

I told her, "I haven't been to the White House since I was invited to lunch there by Ellie Boettiger, whose grandfather was F.D.R. She and I attended the same private girls' school in San Francisco. After lunch she ushered my parents and me around the White House. She pointed to a portrait of her grandfather that had recently been finished.

" 'This is where they're going to hang my grandfather,' I remember Ellie saying.

"After the White House door shut behind us, my father, who was a staunch Republican with a wry sense of humor, could hardly wait to remark, 'It's not where they're going to hang Roosevelt. It's when!' "

Nancy found that hilarious. I also told her I wanted to see the Clement Conger rooms at the State Department. Clement Conger is a great authority on the decorative arts in early America. I had met him when he gave a lecture at the de Young Museum in San Francisco. He was on a tour around the country to appeal to wealthy donors for the funds he needed to acquire antiques to fill the additional rooms. One of my friends (who is a very good friend of his) told me that he had transformed the top floor of the ordinary, rather ugly modern building that houses the State Department into a sort of American Versailles. Like the Versailles Palace outside of Paris, it is used to entertain foreign dignitaries and diplomats. Before Clement Conger performed his miracle, the rooms were a disgrace.

I later found out that Nancy was not on good terms with

Conger. He got along beautifully with Jackie, and it is he who deserved the credit for redecorating the White House during the Kennedy years. His taste and knowledge were extraordinary, but as I said, Nancy and he did not get along. However, I didn't realize this situation when I asked her.

"I'll arrange for you to see the State Department," she offered. "I'll see that you have a private limousine to take you and bring you back. O.K.?"

Nancy and her friends Betsy Bloomingdale and Mary Jane Wick pronounced "O.K." as if the second syllable rhymed with "I." All three of them peppered their conversations with "O.K." at every opportunity. I imagine Nancy must have started it or liked it when she heard someone say it that way. And so the others felt it was chic.

I went to New York on my way to Washington and saw a great many friends. Because I wanted to keep a rather low profile during my time in the capital, I didn't call my friends in Washington to tell them I was coming, nor did I call them during the week I was there.

I did ask Mary Jane Wick for the name of her hairdresser, which she gave me, and then she immediately asked me to lunch. At that time she was serving as liaison between Nancy and me. Usually when Nancy and I had a consultation, we agreed on the next time we would talk. But there were times when I needed to talk to Nancy about matters that came up unexpectedly. I was always careful not to make a habit of going through the White House switchboard or ever leaving my name and phone number with them. When Mary Jane was out of town, I did call the White House occasionally. I would leave a message to "call Joan" with Nancy's social secretary, Elaine Crispin, when Nancy was out or unable to come directly to the phone. But that didn't happen often enough for my call to cause comment or for secrecy to be breached.

Several days after I talked to her, Mary Jane, who had

undoubtedly told Nancy about the luncheon invitation, called and canceled, saying that her husband, Charles Z. Wick, Director of the U.S. Information Agency, had been called out of town the week I would be there and that she had to accompany him. It may have been true, but I doubt it. I rather imagine she got her marching orders from Nancy, who didn't want me to be so much in evidence in Washington. I thought that Nancy, being a worrier, would probably be on pins and needles the entire time I was there.

What Nancy did in the way of providing an escort for the State Dinner only confirmed this to me. Nancy did not offer to let me bring my own escort. She told me during our customary short chat before a consultation, "Everyone I know here is married. I'm going to provide a Marine guard to escort you. I simply don't know any unattached men. O.K.?"

One would have to be very unsophisticated to believe that any hostess of any importance in any big city doesn't have several escorts at her beck and call. Such men are always delighted to fall in with the hostess' plans in return for the social favor of being included in a party.

When courtesy obliges the lady, in this case no ordinary lady but the First Lady, to provide an escort, such men are always available. Their manners are polished and they are agreeable company for one evening. And if the hostess wants to be extra nice, she can usually produce a distinguished or interesting extra man.

As I said before, I knew that she didn't want to make a point of my being there. But I did want to go to Washington at least once while the Reagans were occupying the White House. In January, when I started planning the trip for April, I knew from my stars that it would be a good time for me to go, but I honestly did not anticipate what would happen in the Soviet Union on March 11th.

On March 11, 1985, Mikhail Gorbachev was appointed by the

Central Committee of the Communist Party of the Soviet Union
to succeed the late Konstantin Chernenko as Secretary General
of the U.S.S.R. Long articles were written about Gorbachev in
the newspapers, but a lot of information was missing from the
biographies given. The thoroughly detailed career history that
would have emerged in the case of any newly elected Western
leader of importance was not included, perhaps intentionally.
Many facts concerning his life before he attained his position of
power were not known.

Some of the items our government discovered didn't come
out in the newspapers. For instance, Nancy told me that Gorbachev's mother was a devout practicing Christian. That and a
few other things she told me gave me a better picture of
Gorbachev, the man. Little was known about his wife, Raisa.
Her birthplace, her birthdate, as well as the date of her marriage remain a mystery, even now. To me, as an astrologer, that
would have been of the greatest interest. I always confirmed
events that I wasn't sure of in Ronnie's horoscope by referring to
Nancy's chart.

What interested me most, of course, was Gorbachev's own
birth information. I learned that he had been born March 2,
1931, in Privolnoye, Krasnogvardeisky District, in the Soviet
Union. To me, that was more important than any other portion
of his biography. However, another factor of utmost importance
was missing. To be able to cast up an accurate horoscope, it is
absolutely essential for an astrologer to know the exact time of
day an individual was born. If this is not known or only known
approximately, there are ways of figuring it out. As I've explained previously, this process is called rectification. It is rather
like solving a combination puzzle and mystery. You start with
known factors just as you start solving a puzzle by definitions or
a murder with the available clues.

In Gorbachev's case, the clues I took most into consideration
were his appearance, the fact that he was an intellectual and the

time he had attained his position of power. From that I formed a hypothesis about the placement of the various factors in his horoscope. These I checked out with the other known events of his life to date. I did this mathematically. To countercheck my conclusions, I consulted certain very sensitive additional charts that proved precisely, accurately and conclusively that my detective work and the solution of my puzzle were correct.

The process of rectification is sometimes lengthy and laborious, but, like some scientific discoveries, my rectification of Gorbachev's horoscope came in a flash. Looking back, I now realize that I was helped by certain similarities in the charts of other famous people's horoscopes that I know intimately. I will explain this further and will provide a detailed analysis of the Secretary General's horoscope in a later chapter.

Later events confirmed my rectification conclusively. However, it was not nearly as important an achievement as finishing my comparison of Mikhail Gorbachev's horoscope with that of Ronald Reagan. The comparison indicated that a powerful chemistry would exist between these two great world leaders. The possibilities were breathtaking!

Over the years, I had spent less time in Washington than in New York City, where I had lived, sometimes for extended periods, during the '50s and '60s. The few days I spent in New York on my 1985 trip, I had the feeling that the city was overcrowded, that there were too many people and there was too little time. In Washington, on the other hand, there are so many open areas for strolling, so many beautiful buildings and familiar monuments. While you know a great many people live in and visit Washington, you have the sense not of crowding and pushing and hurrying, but of leisure and space. It is as if the capital absorbs and distributes its inhabitants more graciously than other cities manage to do.

One of my cab drivers told me that in the last twenty years many slum areas have been torn down and replaced with new housing. I had a very upbeat impression of the capital midway through the Reagan years.


## The Welcoming Ceremonies

The morning of the welcoming ceremonies, the security at the White House was tight. I gave the guard my passport for identification and, after being checked out carefully, I was admitted and shown into an anteroom where others were waiting to attend the ceremony on the East Lawn. Most of the people were famous, talented, successful and young. A nice young basketball star bounded over and said hello enthusiastically. He asked if I was a movie star and seemed disappointed when I said no. The pretty slender blonde actress Cheryl Ladd was there with her husband. Joe Namath came over to me and admired the jeweled koala bear and bees I was wearing on my collar. He introduced his new wife, who looked scarcely older than a high school girl.

Nancy's social secretary, Elaine Crispin, was frankly curious. I had deliberately played down my television appearances during the time I was doing the Reagans' astrology, and I was careful not to wear the same dress I had worn during my appearance on the "Merv Griffin Show." When you don't wear the same dress people have seen you in on television, your face is still familiar to them. They know they have seen you somewhere, but they usually can't remember quite where.

I don't think it would have been quite as easy for Elaine not to have known who I was in the Seventies. But in the mid-Eighties, Merv's show had lost popularity and my name was hardly a household word. While something about me obviously tickled Elaine's memory, she couldn't place me and found that faintly disturbing. When she asked what I did, I told her I was a writer and added that I was a staunch Republican from California, but I knew her curiosity hadn't been satisfied.

We had coffee and breakfast pastries and chatted. Bujones, the ballet dancer, was there with lovely Marianna Tcherkassy, his partner for the performance scheduled after the State Dinner the following night. I walked to the ceremony with them. The East Lawn was set up with mini-bleachers, and I was lucky enough to find a seat. The latecomers had to stand.

The ceremony was impressive. There were the flags of both countries and a display of the military. A drill platoon in powdered wigs and pastel-colored Colonial uniforms was a charming reminder of our country's history. The President arrived with Nancy. He made an official welcoming speech, which the Algerian President answered in his own language. When the speeches were over, the crowd dispersed.

### The State Dinner

An official car and driver picked me up at my hotel the evening of April 10th. The young Marine guard who was to escort me introduced himself. Both the driver and the Marine were interested in finding out more about me and why I had been invited. I turned the conversation back to them. The driver, who had made a career of government service, was accustomed to celebrities and foreign dignitaries.

The young Marine had been chosen for White House duty recently after a thorough investigation and having to wait two years to be accepted. He was cleancut, natural and very nice. It was the first time he had escorted anyone to a State Dinner. He was quite obviously impressed to be going and in awe of me.

Quite a few people were ahead of us when we entered the White House. The Marine escort told me that he would meet me after I had walked alone through a room ahead. I could see that every arriving guest or couple had to walk a gauntlet of photographers. People of national importance or international interest faced a blinding barrage of flashbulbs. Others had their pictures taken by photographers sent by newspapers from their own locality. Unlike the people ahead of me, when I walked through that room, I did so without a single flashbulb going off. Nancy quite obviously did not want to make a point of my being there. Everything had been thought out and carefully arranged.

The Marine was waiting for me in the room where cocktails were being served. I didn't see anyone I knew, but I did have several interesting conversations with people I encountered casually. The editor of *Newsweek* was interesting to talk to. He was a tall chap with a shy little wife, who never spoke. Several Algerian diplomats came over and introduced themselves. The Marine, who maintained a respectful silence, told me later how impressed he had been that I knew about their country and *L'Etranger*, a short Camus novel set in Algiers. While I had known that the book was considered a masterpiece, I had never realized its political implications, which the diplomats pointed out and explained to me.

The receiving line had formed, and I could see Nancy ahead looking very glamorous in a pretty red dress by an American designer. I was wearing a pale blue mousseline print by St. Laurent, with an antique red amber Victorian necklace and matching earrings that people often mistake for rubies. While my newest evening dress was red, I deliberately didn't wear it. At that time, red was Nancy's signature color, and recently the style sections of the newspapers had mentioned that the President especially noticed women reporters wearing red.

The name of each person who goes through the receiving line is announced to the President. In person, Ronald Reagan was as handsome as his pictures and every bit as charming and attractive as his television appearances would lead one to believe.

When he heard my name, he smiled, leaned down and kissed me on the cheek.

"Hello, Joan," he said, and greeted me cordially, as if we knew each other already, which in a way we did.

When he shook hands, I said, "Mr. President, I feel that you have been chosen to bring peace." He leaned down to listen. Then he smiled, looked very pleased and thanked me graciously before I passed to the next person in the receiving line.

Nancy was very glamorous in person. "What did you say to Ronnie?" she could hardly wait to ask me. "He looked so pleased!" I told her what I had said. She then complimented me on my dress and necklace, and I told her how pretty her dress was.

There were other people in the receiving line, but I honestly can't recall who they were or having any exchange with them apart from a polite handshake. The Marine guard met me at the end of the line to escort me to the entrance of the room where dinner was to be served on round tables for ten. The flower arrangements were spectacular. Spring flowers with masses of the most beautiful tulips I think I have ever seen.

I was seated at George Bush's table, across from him. The wife of the Algerian President was on his right. I was seated between Cheryl Ladd's husband and the husband of a girl I'd gone to school with in San Francisco. She made a point of coming over to tell me that I'd be sitting next to her husband, and she demanded to know "Why did the President kiss you?" I passed it off by saying, "Well, as you know, my father is a good Republican." That seemed to satisfy her.

George Bush was by far the most interesting person at the table. His dinner partner, the wife of the Algerian President, said very little. Her English was not fluent. So George Bush spoke to me across the table for ten or fifteen minutes.

"I think you won the debate with Geraldine Ferraro, hands down," I said. Debating with the first woman candidate on a national ticket had been a ticklish situation, and Bush had had to tread very carefully between fighting for his ticket and appearing to bully a woman. I felt he had succeeded very well.

I don't remember the rest of our conversation verbatim except that he mentioned the rather vulgar aside he had made to a blue collar worker during a campaign visit shortly after the debate. The remark was overheard by a reporter and had been blown up out of all proportion by the media. George Bush, while he gets along well with all sorts of people, is so obviously a gentleman, I felt at the time that the remark was out of character and beneath him and an attempt for grass roots appeal that didn't ring true. In person, he impressed me as a well-educated, well-bred, intelligent, able, outgoing and charming man.

However, Bush wasn't at that time as confident as I would have expected from my sister's enthusiastic description of him. She had talked with him when he was the Chairman of the Republican National Committee.

I had the impression that occupying the second highest office and living for five years in the President's shadow was not calculated to make anyone feel as confident as occupying the top position. Being Vice-President is at best an "office-in-waiting" and not really suited to giving one's abilities free rein. Loyalty led to his deferring and standing back in a way that I didn't feel was natural to him. Certainly, he didn't have Reagan's populist appeal. I felt he would have liked to have had it, but that he had so much to offer, he was better off being himself.

My memory of the dinner is that the food was excellent. The first course was a seafood mousse followed by a delicious roast veal, both served with very good wines. Champagne was poured with the dessert so that we could all join in the toasts proposed by the President and his guest of honor after their short speeches.

The perfect service, along with the extraordinary flower arrangements I've already mentioned, indicated to me that Nancy was an accomplished hostess who made the most of the considerable resources she commanded as First Lady. And it was a thrill and privilege to meet the President and George Bush and to see my constant phone pal, Nancy, in person for the second time.

After dinner, the President and the First Lady circulated among their guests. As I was leaving the dining room, someone asked me which Reagan I was a friend of. It was rather like having the ushers at a wedding ask you whether you preferred to be seated on the bride's or the groom's side of the aisle. I said I knew Nancy better.

Ronnie came over to talk to me as I was heading toward the area where Nancy was holding court. We had a short conversation. He had apparently liked what I had said to him in the receiving line. And I distinctly remember him saying, "I believe God has chosen me for a mission. God gives me my strength. I've known that all my life."

We could have gone on talking, but people began to crowd around him, eager for his attention, so I joined the group surrounding Nancy. Some woman was trying to convince her to go to her Smith reunion. Nancy told her politely but firmly she wasn't going. I said I didn't intend to go to my Vassar reunion either. We chatted briefly. Nancy said again how much she admired my dress. There were so many people waiting to talk to her, I left to find a seat in the theatre, where the ballet was to begin soon.

While the dancers were superb, the stage was too small for the ballet to be really effective. I talked to the people sitting on either side of me briefly before the performance. They were all friendly, but it would have been a little more fun not to have been alone.

After the entertainment, my Marine came to escort me into a room where there was an orchestra and an area cleared for dancing. Nancy and Ronnie were the first couple on the floor.

They danced together beautifully. George Schultz joined in the dancing with Cheryl Ladd. Couple after couple began to dance.

The Marine guard asked me respectfully if I would dance just one dance with him. "Ma'am, my mother would be so impressed if I could write her that I had danced at a State Dinner at the White House." Of course, I danced with him, and then he took me back to my hotel.

### Tea With Nancy

Except for meeting the President and the man who was going to be President, tea with Nancy was more interesting than the State Dinner. She greeted me downstairs in the White House, and we took a small elevator up to the private quarters the Reagans occupied during both terms.

The weather had turned hot quite abruptly that morning, so I wore a silk outfit I had brought with me instead of a wool tunic I'd also brought. Nancy was very Adolfo with the gold chains, a pretty silk blouse and the suit with the trimmed little jacket.

We immediately started talking and my first impression of the apartment was that it was decorated well and effectively, but it wasn't until Nancy showed me around later that I really had a chance to look.

A tea tray was brought in and placed on a table in front of us. There were two cups of tea and a plate of stale-looking petits fours and some cookies, which neither of us touched. But we did drink the tea. One cup each.

"Ronnie told me last night what you said to him in the receiving line. It pleased him very much." Then she changed the subject. "Do you know what one of the newsmen said to me in the receiving line? He said that if Ronnie were to do nothing more than he has done already, his place in history would be assured."

That was the first time I could remember Nancy mentioning the President's place in history. I made a mental note of it. Now, in retrospect, I think it may have been the birth of an idea that became an obsession later. Being president, of course, guarantees such a place. But there are presidents and presidents, and I think the remark had pleased her mightily and led her to think about such a place being a particularly outstanding one.

Sainthood is the ultimate honor for a Catholic. Even becoming Pope does not assure it. A hint of ambition rules it out. Not so with a place in history, ambition is more often present than not. History rewards ambition. There is no historical devil's advocate to disqualify a pretender. Ambition is not a deterrent; it is a plus.

For a man or woman of action, conscious in life of great importance, motivated by self-aggrandizement to work beyond capacity, to whom, in life, applause means everything, it was a heady prospect—the ultimate achievement—to occupy an enviable place in history after death.

Great figures in history either devote their energies to conquest or dedicate their lives to some great cause. Genghis Khan, Alexander, the Borgias and Medicis, Napoleon, Hitler, Stalin, Mussolini live on in ignominy. But on the other hand, there was the prospect of joining the ranks of Washington, Jefferson, the Adamses, Lincoln, Woodrow Wilson, both Roosevelts, Churchill, de Gaulle, Eisenhower, Victoria and Albert, the Elizabeths, I and II—the list goes on and on.

Nancy was almost totally innocent of history. I was often surprised by how little she knew about it. Highly intelligent, superbly motivated, purposefully organized, she was in no way an intellectual or deeply reflective. But in the same receiving line in which Ronnie had been made aware of his role as peacemaker, Nancy herself had realized that an enviable place in history was not only desirable but within her husband's grasp.

"Did you like the State Dinner?" Nancy asked.

"Quite a change, I imagine, after Rosalynn Carter!" I said. "Your food is excellent. You must have a very special chef." Then I asked her if she planned the menus with him or if she left it to someone else.

"No, I suggest the menus myself. Ronnie and I try out the dinners a few days beforehand. You know how necessary that is. But Ronnie always grumbles about having to eat the same meal twice in such a short time!"

In San Francisco, test dinners were quite usual, especially for gourmet wine and food societies, but I told her that it was usually the wife of the chairman of a dinner who objected to having to attend the same dinner as many as three times before the main event.

Nancy asked me if I had noticed George Schultz dancing with Cheryl Ladd the evening before.

"He looked like he was having a fine time for himself," I said.

"He always does after State Dinners. He loves to dance with all the pretty young glamour girls, the actresses and starlets. He always insists on having his picture taken with the current one. He has the photographer enlarge the photos, and his secretary plasters them all over his office at State. Poor woman has to take them all down and replace them when a new glamour girl comes. It's a sort of joke. Don't you think it's amusing? I do.

"Don't you think Cheryl's pretty?" Nancy asked.

"Very! As you know, I sat next to her husband at dinner. I was rather surprised when he asked me why I hadn't married."

"He shouldn't have. How gauche! Obviously, you have preferred a career. Now all the women's groups are saying I've lived vicariously through Ronnie. They forget I had a successful career as an actress before I ever got married. And it wasn't as ordinary then for a woman to have a career."

"With your stars you were obviously destined for marriage, and a successful one. Except for Ronnie's being elected President, your wedding date was the luckiest day in your life." I asked her if she could remember the time of the wedding, but she said she could only remember the date.

"I felt as if my life really began with my marriage. You know, having a husband, being a married woman with my own home, children. That meant much more to me than any career."

I had to smile. What Nancy had just said was so typical of her horoscope. I told her that, then added, "It amused me so much when I talked to Ronnie after dinner, and he told me that he felt God had entrusted him with a mission and that his strength came directly from God. What he said was almost word for word like a passage out of my book, *Astrology for Adults*, describing Jupiter in Scorpio. As I've told you, Nancy, Jupiter is a very important planet in Ronnie's chart."

"Tell me again exactly what you said to Ronnie in the receiving line. You've no idea how pleased he was!"

"I said I believed he had been chosen to bring peace." I didn't go into what I had seen in Gorbachev's horoscope. The time was not right. I was holding that in reserve. But the idea had been planted and, from what Nancy said, had taken root.

"Tell me," she said, "what did you think of George Bush?"

"I was very impressed by him, actually. I calculated his chart during the 1980 primaries, but of course Ronnie's stars showed that it was his time to win. I'm practically certain that Bush will be our next president."

Nancy didn't agree. "He's a nice man and very capable. But he's no Ronnie. He comes across as a 'wimp.' "

I'd heard the term, of course, but I'd never thought of its being associated with George Bush. Later on, it was to haunt him, and the Democrats did use it against him, but of course he overcame that.

"I don't think he can make it," Nancy said. "He's a nice man, but his image is against him. It isn't macho enough."

I liked Bush, and I said that I thought his image could be improved when he has a chance to express himself more fully and that while Bush was of course very different from Ronnie, I believed he would overcome the "wimp" image she had mentioned and win.

We'd been so busy talking, I hadn't had a chance to look around. As I began taking in the room around me I became aware that Nancy was very concerned about the upcoming trip to Germany, a place called Bitburg and someone she kept referring to as "that man."

Before I left San Francisco, I'd seen in my charts the possibility of a controversy or scandal in Washington around this time. Before my trip to Washington, I had heard the President tell a press conference that he would not visit the site of a concentration camp during his upcoming visit to Germany. He felt that it was time to put old bitternesses behind us and go forward with the problems at hand.

Since I had arrived in the East, I'd been so busy seeing friends in New York, visiting the museums in Washington, and touring the White House and the State Department that I had not been reading the newspapers. And so I did not know that the controversy over the Reagan's visit to Germany was escalating and beginning to get out of hand.

As you may remember, the Reagans were planning to visit the cemetery in the village of Bitburg and lay a wreath to honor the German dead. Nancy explained that it was essential to make the gesture because it was vital to us that Kohl be reelected. His party, unlike his opposition, would allow us to place missiles in Germany. For this reason, Kohl's remaining in power was essential to the success of Reagan's grand strategy to protect Europe from Russian aggression and to be able to deal with the new Russian leader from a position of strength.

I knew, of course, that before the President went anywhere a team was sent out to study the security situation and to prepare for the upcoming visit. They planned the schedule, coped with the details and made all the necessary arrangements. This was usually done well in advance. In this case, the team had made its investigation during the winter. By spring, it was discovered that there were graves of Nazi World War II soldiers in the Bitburg cemetery, which our people hadn't known about because at the time of their investigation the graves were covered with snow.

It is only common sense to realize that it would be hard if not impossible to find a cemetery anywhere in Germany that did not contain a single Nazi grave. Bitburg had blown up into such a controversial issue in Germany that if Reagan now refused to lay a wreath as planned originally, Kohl's government would most surely be defeated at the polls.

"It's that man," Nancy kept repeating. "He acts like he's crazy. It's his fault. He's a fanatic." She repeated over and over the phrase "that man."

At the time, I knew very little about Elie Wiesel. When I returned to my hotel, I read the newspaper and discovered that Elie Wiesel was a German Jew who had survived Auschwitz, the concentration camp where his father had died. Elie was later transferred to Buchenwald. He had written with great sensitivity about unspeakable horrors. What he had lived through had been so intolerable he could never put it behind him. Certain human experiences cut open wounds that can never heal. In the article I read, he was quoted as saying, "It is a Jewish tradition to speak the truth to power." In that spirit, he was protesting the gesture the President was planning to make. Anyone reading about what Elie Wiesel had lived through must understand why Reagan's proposed visit to Bitburg was abhorrent to him. But when I was having tea with Nancy, I did not know what Elie Wiesel had suffered.

To be fair, Nancy was not a religious bigot. She liked her wealthy Jewish friends as well as her friends of other religions. It was more a matter of social position and manners. Jews who made a protest like Elie Wiesel annoyed her as did anyone else who stood in her way.

Nor was Nancy insensitive. At times, her sensitivity to her own feelings bordered on self-pity. Her feelings for Ronnie were unquestionably deep and sincere. Her intuitions about the people surrounding him were almost preternaturally acute. And she was dedicated to protecting her husband and serving his interests above all else.

Her insights into the desires and motives of others were equally sharp. They enabled her to use and manipulate people for her own purposes. However, she avoided doing favors even when it would have been very easy for her. She did the minimum necessary to persuade people to do what she wanted done.

When Nancy talked about people, even people very close to her, she always got a little dig in. However, when she spoke about Ronnie, it was either to make his idiosyncrasies endearingly human or to praise him. To her, he was not only loveable, he was likeable. Nancy was not alone in this. From the polls still being taken, the majority of Americans still feel that way.

Abruptly, the conversation about Bitburg turned to lighter subjects. "Your flower arrangements are spectacular," I told her. "I've never seen such magnificent tulips anywhere."

Nancy was pleased that I had noticed. She said, "I supervise all the flower arrangements myself."

"The White House is very different from the way it looked when I had lunch with Ellie," I said. "It's so elegant now. Then, as I remember, it was plain and rather barnlike in places. But I was only a schoolgirl and didn't pay much attention to such things."

"I've tried to make some other changes," Nancy said, "but Clement Conger is very difficult."

"But you do have to admit that the collection of Americana at State is wonderful," I said, and thanked her for the car.

I also told Nancy about my visit to the Freer Galleries to see the Chinese ceramics. Although they are considered the gems of the collection, I had seen them before, and this visit, it was the Whistlers that captivated me. In art history, I'd seen slides of the "Study in Black and Gray," popularly known as "Whistler's Mother." But I'd never before seen Whistlers in color. The Freer has two rooms of them, and they are exquisite. I had never realized how abstract and modern Whistler was, even though his subjects were representational. I liked the aura of peace and the quiet intimacy of the Whistler canvases. They were rather like a philosophical treatise in paint.

I also told Nancy about the Air and Space Museum, where you can see the history of flight in America illustrated by actual models of famous planes. The Wright brothers are represented. Lindberg's *Spirit of St. Louis* as well as the first lunar module are all in that remarkable museum. I went back to visit it twice.

Nancy was very interested in my descriptions of both museums. "I'm like a prisoner. I can hardly go anywhere," she said, then added rather pitifully, "I never get to go to galleries or museums. It's too difficult with the Secret Service. They would have to clear everyone else out."

"I guess everything has its advantages and disadvantages," I said. "But how many people have your experience? So incredibly few. You have to think of that."

After chatting a few more minutes, I decided it was time to leave. Nancy seemed to me a little lonesome. She acted as if she would like to delay my departure.

"Let me show you around," she offered.

The Reagan quarters were nicely decorated with many artfully arranged ornaments. Her decorator had created a pleasing effect. The Tang camel was magnificent, and I commented on it particularly.

"I found it in the basement of the White House," Nancy said. "I like it, but of course when we leave, I'll have to give it back."

At the elevator door, I thanked Nancy, and she thanked me for coming. Then, as I stood facing her, I caught myself making a comparison. I remembered seeing Jackie in person in New York in the early Sixties. Yet while Nancy and Jackie have entirely different features, I was struck by their having the same massive bony facial structure that photographs so exceptionally well.

I tend to become very fond of the people I know as intimately as I knew Nancy and to accept them as they are. On my part, a feeling of friendship had developed because of the shared experiences and because of our close and constant work for common goals.

When you talk on the phone with someone as frequently as I had talked to Nancy, you get to know her thoroughly. I also had the advantage of being able to refer to her horoscope and to understand her from an astrological point of view. Nevertheless, as well as you know someone by phone or from reading her horoscope, there is an added dimension when you talk with her in person and spend time together in the same room.

I pressed the elevator button. Nancy hugged me and kissed me on the cheek. Then, for some reason I can't quite put my finger on, I had the oddest impression. Nancy had just made a warm and affectionate gesture. Yet I can remember thinking, "This woman could chew someone up and swallow and spit out the bones and never feel a thing."

# X

# Defusing Bitburg

You have seen from the last chapter how the Bitburg controversy was growing during my visit to Washington in early April 1985. By the time I arrived back in San Francisco, it was beginning to get out of hand. Nancy called me sometimes several times daily. It was a real dilemma. On the one hand, there was an outcry from people who rallied around Elie Wiesel; sentiment was also running very high in Germany, and there was the specter of Kohl's government falling if the President's promise to visit the Bitburg cemetery was not fulfilled. Kohl was committed to allowing our missiles to be based in Germany, and his loss would gravely undermine Reagan's grand strategy in Europe, which hopefully would permit him to deal with the new Russian leader from a position of strength.

Knowing of the suffering, not only of Jews but of Catholic priests and others, one could not help but sympathize with their point of view. As the leader of the free world and a country

118

founded on idealistic principles, Reagan was a living symbol, an example for all men and women of good will. When he appeared anywhere, he honored that place with his presence and dignified it with his speech. It was no wonder that it was abhorrent to Elie Wiesel and others, many of them not Jewish, for Ronald Reagan to lay a wreath in a cemetery that contained even one Nazi grave. So much importance rode on that one gesture. I gave it a great deal of thought. There was a consensus that the Reagans should honor the memory of the Jews and others who had been tortured and murdered or else damaged psychologically for life at Bergen-Belsen, a German concentration camp.

Nancy called and asked me if I would time both visits, to Bergen-Belsen and to Bitburg. Mike Deaver had proposed a schedule to her, but, as usual, she relied on my ability to solve problems and give sound advice. She knew that my expert timing could save the day for Ronnie. And so it did.

Before even starting on the astrology, I made a policy decision about my overall goals. This was my reasoning. Laying a wreath at Bergen-Belsen must be the most important gesture. The controversy surrounding the wreath-laying at the Bitburg cemetery made it imperative that it be done as quickly and inconspicuously as possible, given the world attention the proposed visit had already attracted.

Both visits were planned for May 5, 1985. I chose the very conspicuous and highly visible time of 11:45 A.M. for Bergen-Belsen. When the majority of the planets in a chart are placed above the line that divides the circle of a chart in two horizontally, the event is very much in the limelight. At the time I chose, the Sun, which ruled the event itself, was in a very elevated position in the 10th house of great prominence and prestige. The Sun and the proud, noble, honorable and dignified Leo Ascendant described the nature of the event. Jupiter, the planet of benevolence and good will, represented the public. Two planets in the 9th house indicated global attention. And Mars in the 10th showed a kind of victory. The Moon going into conjunction with a Scorpio Saturn in the 4th house of the grave emphasized the memory of the holocaust horror and the warning that no one must suffer so tragically again.

This chart satisfied every requirement. It was prominent and highly visible. The message I thought it proper to deliver was described perfectly by the chart. The publicity it would attract would be great, and the warning (the fixed sign of Scorpio describes permanence) would be remembered by all who witnessed it for a long time to come. The fixed sign of Leo rising ruled by the Sun in the fixed sign of Taurus reinforced this.

I planned that the visit to the Bitburg cemetery would be as inconspicuous as possible under the circumstances, that it would last as short a time as the motion of laying a wreath would take, preferably ten minutes at most. At a time when the planets representing the public perception of an event are in favorable configuration, even sworn enemies tend to agree. I added another astrological element which means that nothing much happens and one's worst worries never come to pass. The cardinal signs get things over with quickly and people go on to something else. The Moon and Saturn in the Third house described the visit to the cemetary while the position of Jupiter indicated the brief ceremony that took place. Neptune on the angle of the chart veiled the occasion and dimmed it. The time I chose was 2:45 P.M.

Mike Deaver's tentative plans turned out to be so different from mine that Nancy had trouble turning from the phone to Mike to tell him what I wanted to do about timing. "I can't go back and forth between the two of you. It's impossible!" she said. I could imagine her throwing up her hands in disgust and handing over the receiver. She put Mike on the phone with me and told him to do what I said.

Mike told me that they had planned their visit to Bitburg for the morning. I said, "Wrong," and told him to change it to the afternoon at my chosen time. I gave him the late morning time for Bergen-Belsen and advised a long ceremony.

The only difficulty was that someone had planned for the Reagans to have an hour-long picnic with the villagers at Bitburg, which I said was absolutely out of the question as it made Bitburg far too important and called attention to something I felt should be glossed over rapidly.

The only remaining trouble was the schedule. It was too late to alter it completely for logistical reasons. Mike was so eager to get out of the mess he was in, he was willing to do anything I said. I told him that the picnic had to be cancelled. I suggested that the Reagan plane fly around in circles as long as it had to in order to land at Bitburg at my chosen time.

Mike breathed a sigh of relief. He was always very efficient in carrying out the instructions I usually relayed through Nancy. It was the only time I talked to him directly while he was at the White House. After he left the White House, he did call me when he was being investigated by Congress for lobbying activities. Nancy had suggested that I would be able to help him out. At the time he called, I already had more work than I could handle, so I was unable to take him on as a client.

Mike carried out my orders. The Bergen-Belsen visit was long and visible. Between the two visits, the plane circled as long as it had to. The Bitburg visit was brief, and the controversy soon died down. I had defused Bitburg for all intents and purposes.

Kohl was reelected, and the missiles were installed in Germany. And the stage was set for President Reagan to go into his first meeting with the new Secretary General of Russia, Mikhail Gorbachev. His grand strategy in Europe firmly in place, the President would now be able to deal with the Soviet leader from a position of strength.

# XI

# Analysis of President Mikhail Gorbachev's Horoscope

I have already explained that it is necessary for an astrologer to know the exact time of day an individual was born to calculate an accurate horoscope. If the time is not known, the astrologer has to figure it out by working backwards from known events of the individual's life and other clues, such as personal appearance, health problems and psychological characteristics.

However, when there is no hint of an approximate hour, rectification can be very difficult and time consuming, even for an expert astrologer. Merely knowing whether it was night or day would be a help and eliminate many puzzling possibilities.

With President Reagan's chart, when no time of birth was

known, there were as many speculative birthtimes as there were astrologers speculating about it. It took many hours of patient work before I was satisfied that I had arrived at Ronald Reagan's birthtime perfectly, to the exact second.

Not so with Gorbachev. Again, I only had the date and place of birth. Much less was known about him. The date of his marriage, his children's births, information an astrologer normally would use, were missing. However, the few clues I did have clicked! I was able to rectify Gorbachev's horoscope in a flash. In many years of practicing astrology, no rectification has been easier.

As in the moment a scientific discovery is made, some faculty higher than the human mind enables one to take a giant leap between not knowing and knowing. At the time, my almost instant rectification of Gorbachev's horoscope seemed like a miracle.

When Gorbachev had been chosen Secretary General of the U.S.S.R. on March 11, 1985, a configuration in his horoscope described his realizing his hopes and wishes through fantastically important friends acting in his interest. I have seen similar indications in the charts of other famous men in history. The clue that meant most to me, however, was the newspaper report describing him as an intellectual.

In astrology, Mercury, the planet of the mind, describes an intellectual, a person whose powers are primarily mental. In the past, astrologers never regarded Mercury as the most vital planet for leadership. Why then is it a fact that Mercury is the most important planet not only in Gorbachev's chart but in the charts of so many contemporary world leaders?

The reason Mercury has become so important in modern times in the horoscopes of leaders is that Mercury gives the power to understand and communicate ideas, an ability so essential for any dominant political figure. A modern leader, for success, must above all have a genius for communicating through the media.

Reagan, of course, immediately comes to mind because he has been called "the great communicator." However, while Reagan is intelligent, he does not come across as an intellectual. His genial manner, optimistic outlook and his reassuring presence make people think that he is truly nice, a really decent human being. At times, Reagan can plan like a great general. He is a man of action, not a thinker.

The two most important planets in Gorbachev's chart are his Mercury in Aquarius and his Sun in Pisces. An Aquarius Mercury indicates a person fascinated by human behavior. He understands people perfectly. He is rarely deceived about anyone's character or motivation. He loves literature. He loves culture. He especially loves ideas. Above all, Gorbachev is a man of extraordinary insight and vision.

Sun in Pisces can be very strong. Pisces force is spiritual. The Pisces person, typically, is compassionate and self-sacrificing. The Tarot card that represents this sign shows a man, crucified upside down, pouring what is his most valuable asset, a bag of gold coins, on the earth below him. The Pisces person comes into life to benefit others. Yet he is a pragmatist who knows the world. Either he is or he becomes sophisticated. Pisces people are usually lovable. Pisces planets make politicians popular.

The Pisces Sun and Aquarius Mercury in Gorbachev's chart symbolize his mission in this world. Pisces' symbol is the fish. It is also the symbol of the early Christians. The Age of Pisces was dominated by the great religions, including Christianity and Buddhism. Aquarius, sign of the New Age to come, is not a religious sign but one of great humanitarian vision. While an Aquarian leader holds himself aloof from the crowd, he has friends in all walks of life and is very democratic. Of the two pivotal planets in President Gorbachev's horoscope, the Pisces Sun represents the past Age, the Aquarian Mercury represents the Age we are entering. Gorbachev's destiny, his being chosen to lead one of the most powerful nations in the world, makes him a meaningful link between the past and future.

The military force Gorbachev now commands contributes to his being more powerful by far than the Czars of all the Russias past. Because the two planets I've described are at the very apex of his chart, the power they describe is enormous.

Gorbachev is very tough. His Saturn in Capricorn describes someone who may have been a timid child but who in maturity dominates his environment. These people won't back down for anyone. They are self-willed and unyielding.

Pluto's relationship to Saturn in the chart describes a character of immense stubbornness and complexity, but most of all, in Gorbachev's life, it indicates that his worst problem will be the economic conditions in the Soviet Union. Such terrible problems are shown. It is frightening. When I first saw this horoscope, I thought of his country's military expenditures and the economic deprivation of the people. I thought that Gorbachev could be persuaded to lighten up the military load, spending instead on a better living standard for his people. From everything that was shown in his chart, I believed that he could be convinced that this was the path foreordained for him.

What I saw in his chart later turned out to be glasnost and perestroika, or openness (transparency) and economic reform (restructuring). He introduced these two programs in the Soviet Union after the Geneva Summit. It wasn't exactly freedom and free enterprise, but it was a step in the right direction. And it was typical of his horoscope, as you have seen, and an attempt to solve his worst problem.

There is a lot of Gemini in this chart. Gemini people can either be shallow and frivolous or loyal and idealistic, but what is indicated in Gorbachev's natal horoscope is versatility. Gemini is a masculine sign that often indicates executive ability. Gemini can be powerful and dominant at best. But it thrives on variety and hates being tied down to routine work. People with strong Gemini influences in their charts get very restless when forced to confine their activities to one location. They like to have a change of scene, or go on weekend jaunts or experience the intellectual stimulus of travel.

Gemini is, above all, logical, and you really have to watch out when you match your wits with this sort of person. He can argue on either side of a question with equal eloquence; whichever side, he argues with conviction. It is up to you to figure out the basic assumption behind his brilliant argument, and convince him it is wrong, before you can win over such a person to your way of thinking.

The Gemini influence makes people terribly talkative. Before Geneva, I told Nancy that Gorbachev would be a voluble and eager conversationalist. My accuracy in this respect was confirmed later on when the Reagans got to know the Russian leader better. Evidently, as is so typical of the Gemini influence, in this case his rising sign, he talks a lot and even interrupts when a pertinent idea occurs to him suddenly in the course of what someone else is saying. But he doesn't mind at all if someone interrupts him during a conversation for the same reason. He likes to exchange ideas. He loves words and ideas, and when someone talks, he is willing to listen.

Because of a Venus in Capricorn, Gorbachev likes to get something in return from the person to whom he offers his love. He would have wanted to be sure before he asked Raisa to marry him that his offer would be accepted. In the woman of his choice, he would prefer strength of character to mere physical beauty. But the wife who would come to him would be very much on his side, rather fond of luxury and somewhat extravagant but quite lucky. Severe publicly, she would be emotional and demonstrative in private.

With his Moon in Leo, the women in his life would be proud, noble, dignified, particular in dress and rather autocratic. His mother would have been ambitious for him and encouraged him to make the most of his potential. From his horoscope, he would have been unusually attached to his mother.

Because his Jupiter is in Cancer, the Sun Sign of the July 4, 1776, chart of the U.S.A., he would be well received in America, and from the viewpoint of this astrologer, cordial relations with Americans were to be expected.

Mars also in Cancer describes someone creative in action. Cancer is a sign that gets its way—like the active ocean waves that eat away at rocks so unobtrusively that, while the shoreline is altered drastically with the passage of time, one hardly notices the change while it is happening. This isn't the strongest sign for Mars and is more desirable for a creative person than for a man of action. However, it is strongly placed in his chart, which reinforces it and makes it sturdier.

Moon in the best aspect to an Aries Uranus gives Gorbachev originality and dash, a tremendous flair for leadership and formidable charisma. Neptune in Virgo might make him subscribe to the work ethic himself, but he would have trouble with people who didn't like to work; and problems with his people's addiction to alcohol and drugs could undermine his best efforts. All kinds of criminal activity are shown that could prove insidious and weaken the very foundations of his government. Corrupt friends are a very great danger to him, and he should beware of them.

In 1990, Gorbachev is definitely going to have troubles with the military establishment in the Soviet Union. He, himself, is a decent man, but I am not at all sure that the Russian generals are of his opinion or that they agree with his policies. I pray that he is strong enough. One thing I'm sure of is that, in the not too far distant future, his strength will surely be tested.

Two things are going on in Gorbachev's chart that make me very apprehensive. In coming years, Saturn, Uranus and Neptune, the most malevolent planets, will pass over the most troublesome area of his horoscope to challenge him with virtually insoluble economic problems. He will be tested many times in the coming decade. Physical assassination is not an impossibility. In 1989, he has had terrible upsets with friends. These came suddenly and unexpectedly. They are going to continue.

Lenin, leader of the 1917 Revolution and founder of the U.S.S.R., studied not only the writings of Karl Marx but also the political organization of the Roman Catholic Church before he set up the infrastructure of Communist Russia. A church that had lasted for the better part of 2,000 years suggested to him the permanence he desired. When Gorbachev took over in 1985, Russian society had been frozen like a solid block of ice for the better part of the century.

Partially I based what I said to the Reagans about the Russian leader's horoscope on what I first saw in it. I described a man who was tough—he had to be to get to the position he occupied—but highly intelligent, open to new ideas and with the Aquarian vision of the brotherhood of man that he shared with Ronald Reagan. There was a formidable chemistry between the two men's horoscopes, one which I then believed could change the face of modern Russia and relieve the world of the threat of nuclear disaster between the superpowers.

Later, I will tell you of my pride in what I suggested to the President through Nancy after I had read Gorbachev's horoscope for the first time. Now I fear that the wheels I set in motion may run uncontrolled into tragedy because as you will see, advice I gave later may have been ignored. As has happened so many times before, the dream of peace, now so visible, could disappear like a mirage as one approaches it. The present trend of events in the U.S.S.R. is frightening to me, and I pray to God that Gorbachev will be strong enough, lucky enough and wise enough to navigate safely through them.

# XII

# The Chemistry Between Ronald Reagan and Mikhail Gorbachev

Having described separately these two great leaders' horoscopes, it is of particular interest to compare them. I did this carefully before I set out to convince Nancy of my findings.

To begin with, there was a magnificent interchange between the two rising signs. The rising sign of a horoscope is based on the exact time of birth. It tells about the individual himself, his psychological characteristics and his physical body. This Ascendant, or rising sign, is also called "the First house."

The Seventh house, which is directly opposite the First, is the person's opposite, his wife or some other form of partner. The person described by the Seventh house can also be an adversary or open enemy or the other party to an agreement.

When one person's First house is someone else's Seventh, this can indicate that they are a very compatible couple or business partners who cooperate perfectly and complement each other. This interchange between Reagan's and Gorbachev's charts described very friendly enemies who had the joint potential of working together successfully. This astrological interchange is classically a very big plus for any two people working together amicably and cooperating.

The next most significant coming together of planets between the two charts was the placement of Gorbachev's most important planet, Mercury, in Aquarius, Ronald Reagan's Sun Sign. That these two men were destined to communicate and exchange ideas and come to a mutually arrived at vision was predestined. The most important part of that vision, shared by both men, was the idea of some form of mutual disarmament and peace between the two superpowers. Another important part of the equation was that Ronald Reagan had the potential of convincing Gorbachev of modern economic realities. Financial matters were one of the areas where the President's beliefs were sure to influence the Soviet leader. Humanitarian measures, a more democratic U.S.S.R. and freedom from the threat of war, of course, were primary matters for discussion, all of them typically Aquarian.

What I saw in the area of mental compatibility between the two men was confirmed by Reagan's Mercury, the planet of ideas and the mind, very close to Gorbachev's Venus. Both planets were in Capricorn. Venus is the planet of love, Mercury, the planet of ideas. This meant that Gorbachev would love and embrace the ideas the American president would bring him. These two planets, one Ronnie's, the other Gorbachev's, were also in an economic department of Gorbachev's horoscope, and so some economic accommodation between the two countries was to be expected. This gave me the idea of Reagan convincing Gorbachev to alter the Russian economy along principles more resembling free enterprise.

Both the idea of peace and a revised Russian economic structure would be encouraged to result from the meeting of these two men. The personal affection between them was extraordinary. With a man and woman, a coming together of the planet Uranus in one chart with the Venus (or love planet) in the other can be described most aptly as "love at first sight." With two heterosexual men, it is like a terrific chemistry between them, one that is compatible, mutually stimulating and full of good humor. I expected that these two men not only would exchange serious ideas but that they would also laugh together and tell amusing stories. That was the most natural and delightful way for them to make a point, one with the other. (In an article in *The New York Times* on August 21, 1987, Steven Roberts described Reagan's penchant for storytelling:

"You know I have a recent hobby," the President remarked in a speech on economic matters earlier this month. "I have been collecting stories that I can tell, or prove are being told by the citizens of the Soviet Union among themselves, which display not only a sense of humor but their feeling about their system."

Mr. Reagan then told his current favorite, about a Russian who wants to buy a car.

The man goes to the official agency, puts down his money and is told that he can take delivery of this automobile in exactly ten years.

"Morning or afternoon?" the purchaser asks. "Ten years from now, what difference does it make?" replies the clerk.

"Well," says the car-buyer, "the plumber's coming in the morning."

Reporters traveling with him in the 1984 campaign grew thoroughly tired of the one about the commissar who is visiting a Soviet potato farm.

The party official asks a farmer how things are going, and the farmer replies that the harvest is so bountiful that the potatoes would reach the "foot of God" if piled on top of one another.

"But this is the Soviet Union," says the commissar, "there is no God here." The farmer replies, "That's all right, there are no potatoes either.")

Because Ronnie's Mars, the planet of forcefulness, was in such a good relationship with Gorbachev's Neptune, the planet of charm, they would not indulge in the sort of crude bombast that had typified Khrushchev when he came face to face with his American counterpart, Richard Nixon, in Moscow. The Reagan-Gorbachev interchange would be polite, and both would behave generally in a civilized fashion.

Another indication of the formidable mutual affection in the two men's charts was a coming together of Venus in Reagan's chart with Gorbachev's Pisces Sun, the most powerful testimony in these charts of a sympathetic and loving friendship.

There is something I hesitate to mention about Ronald Reagan's horoscope because it might seem unscientific to people who do not understand the spiritual tradition of astrology. However, I venture this observation for the third of the world's population who believe in reincarnation. This belief, which is considered superstitious and nonsensical by the other two-thirds, is even now being confirmed by clinical psychologists and hypnotists who, during attempts to cure some psychological ill that began in childhood, have accidentally regressed patients back to former lives. There are many instances of this.

When in an astrological chart, the house or department of life that indicates the past incarnation is in the same sign as the

Ascendant or rising sign (which signifies the present life), this means that the person has left unfinished something begun in a former incarnation. In this life, the person has returned to complete it. Ronald Reagan is a prime example. He is a man with a mission. It shows in so many places in his horoscope. That this mission originated in the past is evident to any astrologer acquainted with the spiritual meaning of a horoscope.

The friendship that developed between Reagan and Gorbachev in this life is the continuation of a friendship from the past. At their Geneva meeting, I knew they would get along as easily as if they'd known each other before. I firmly believed this.

The relation of Gorbachev's Sun to Reagan's Moon is added proof of their compatibility. As I've explained previously, a favorable relation of the Sun in one chart to the Moon in another often makes people soul mates. It can happen between husband and wife, mother and daughter, father and son, between every kind of relative and between friends totally without blood ties. It means that the two people see eye to eye and have a sympathetic attitude toward one another. The Moon person (in this case Reagan) complements the Sun person (Gorbachev).

But Gorbachev would have a natural respect for Reagan because Reagan's Taurus Moon, so descriptive of his personality or image, shows him to be a very likeable and genial man, but a stubborn one. Quite typical was the way Reagan put his foot down and wouldn't budge an inch when Gorbachev tried to limit SDI at Reykjavik.

# XIII

# The Geneva Summit

**Changing Ronald Reagan's "Evil Empire" Attitude**

*New York Times*, March 9, 1983:
REAGAN DENOUNCES IDEOLOGY OF SOVIET AS
"FOCUS OF EVIL"
Orlando, Fla.: Byline Francis X. Clines

President Reagan, denouncing Soviet Communism as "the focus of evil in the modern world," today warned Protestant church leaders not "to treat the arms race as a giant misunderstanding and thereby remove yourself from the struggle between right and wrong, good and evil."

Appearing before a convention of evangelical Christians, the President delivered one of the most forceful speeches of his administration on the subjects of theology and war, morality and government.

In what White House aides privately said was something
of a rebuttal to recent criticism of Administration policy by
church officials, notably the Roman Catholic hierarchy,
Mr. Reagan delighted his audience by declaring:

"In your discussion of the nuclear freeze proposals, I
urge you to beware the temptation of pride—the temptation of blithely declaring yourselves above it all and label
both sides equally at fault, to ignore the facts of history and
the aggressive impulses of an evil empire." . . . Americans
must not forget that Communists "are the focus of evil in
the modern world."

*Washington Post*, November 20, 1983

President Reagan suggested in a magazine interview
released this week that he never called the Soviet Union
an "evil empire."

Asked by *U.S. News & World Report* how he could
expect the Soviet Union to negotiate an arms-control
agreement "after you've denounced them as liars and
cheats who run an evil empire," Reagan said, ". . . those
weren't my words." He added, "I was only reciting what
they had said . . ."

He apparently confused a March 8, 1983 speech to the
National Association of Evangelicals with an answer to a
question at a January 1981 News Conference.

In the speech to the Evangelicals, Reagan called the
Soviet Union an "evil empire."

At the news conference, he said the Soviets have re-
served the right ". . . to lie, to cheat. . . ."

A White House spokesman later said that Reagan, in
saying "those aren't my words," was referring to the "liars
and cheats" phrase. As for the term "evil empire," deputy

press secretary Bob Sims said Reagan "would not deny that he used that term."

In my first conversation with Nancy concerning the Geneva Summit, her attitude toward the Soviet leader Ronald Reagan was to meet for the first time at Geneva was anything but promising. "Gorbachev is a terrible man," she said. "He's really tough. He has the KGB. Those Russian leaders are practically like gangsters. Ronnie will have to deal with him accordingly." It was obvious to me that what I was hearing from Nancy reflected her husband's opinions.

I began by agreeing with her. "Gorbachev is tough," I said. "It shows in his horoscope. But you don't need astrology to tell you that Gorbachev had to be tough to get to be Secretary General. Nevertheless," I told her, "he is the first open-minded man with humanitarian predilections to occupy his position since Communism began in Russia.

"In the first place," I said, "Gorbachev was born into a different generation than his immediate predecessors. He's a modern man. He doesn't fit into the stereotype. What I see in his horoscope is promising. I think Ronnie can deal with him successfully if he goes about it the right way."

As you will recall, the Soviet leaders during Reagan's first term—Brezhnev, Andropov and Chernenko—were sick old men. Chernenko had died less than a year after he took office. The summit had been postponed several times during Reagan's first term because of Chernenko's ill health. With his death and Gorbachev's ascension to power, a summit became possible. What Nancy had said about previous Russian leaders, I had to admit, had been for the most part correct.

Stalin, like so many of the others, had been an arch criminal. Yet because of an incident during my only trip to the U.S.S.R., I had some hope that there was a wish for peace and cooperation among some of the leaders and the people. I told Nancy about it.

It was fall of 1967. I had gone to Moscow via Paris, Rome and Leningrad. In Paris, a writer I met had been friends with Yuri Zukhov, a Russian journalist who had lived for a time in the West before returning to the U.S.S.R. to become editor of *Pravda*. The writer gave me an introduction to Zukhov. I presented his letter, but I was told that Zukhov was out of the country. That was as close as I came to officialdom in Russia.

In Moscow, as I and my friends were queuing up in front of Lenin's tomb, a shabbily dressed old man left the line and approached us. Proudly he showed us an identification card. The guide told us it proved that he was a veteran of the Revolution. The guide, a chap in his mid-thirties, was obviously embarrassed by the older man's coming over to us. He tried to dismiss him as a garrulous old pest, but the veteran was not to be put off. He persisted until the guide was forced to translate his remarks to get rid of him.

" 'The Russian people don't want war,' he said. 'We want to be friends with the Americans.' " He extended his hand, and all four of us returned his smile and shook hands with him.

After showing us Lenin's tomb, the guide took us to visit the graves of other deceased notables buried in the grounds surrounding the main mausoleum. In an inconspicuously placed plot, next to the grave of an obscure general, Stalin was buried beneath a modest stone marker. Compared to the great tomb he originally occupied, he rested in a deceased Moscovite's equivalent of "Outer Siberia." Some years ago, I remember having heard that he had been reinstated and his grave transferred to a better location.

But curiously enough, for a time, even the Russians had to admit that Stalin was a mass murderer comparable to Hitler. It has been estimated that his victims were in the millions. It may be different now; I'm not sure. But in the late Sixties, he was definitely out of favor, and the government guides had been instructed to make this clear to tourists.

"But what makes you think that a man who can command the KGB is less evil than a Stalin?" Nancy asked.

I said, "I am certain that most of the Russian leaders of the past were repressive and ruthless. Many of them were crude and cruel men. However, Gorbachev's chart leads me to believe that he is different. The placement of his ruler, Mercury, in the Tenth house of power and position convinces me that Gorbachev came to power not only because he had been favored by powerful older men, but also because of his high degree of intelligence. It symbolizes to me that despite his Russian training and origins, he has the instincts of a humanitarian, that he, like Ronnie, is a man of truly remarkable vision.

"Mercury in Aquarius likes ideas. Gorbachev's openness to new ideas is phenomenal!" I repeated this many times in different ways in an effort to convince her.

I told Nancy I had always believed that peace was possible. In the past, it was the conventional wisdom that what led to war was part of human nature and was unalterable. But slavery had once been regarded as the inevitable consequence of human nature, coupled as it was with the belief that some people were naturally inferior. Slavery was outlawed by the British in the early 19th century. Lincoln signed the Emancipation Proclamation on January 1, 1863. Gradually people were weaned from the idea, so that now, while a type of slavery exists in places like South Africa, it is frowned on by the rest of the international community. Those who think that owning the equivalent of slaves is reasonable and right are in a shrinking minority.

Even as I talked to Nancy for three hours—it was the longest session we ever had—I had in my mind that some day war would be like slavery. I knew it would not disappear overnight, or even in our lifetimes. Yet I visualized a day when war would be stamped out like smallpox. I could imagine a future time when school children growing up would regard the history of past wars as archaic and irrelevant to their lives as ancient Greek and Latin.

Nancy was always open to my ideas. She respected them. She felt they had merit. Sometimes she would argue a point repeatedly, but when I was sure of something I saw in the configurations of the planets, I would be unshakable and firm. When I was absolutely certain that a thing was right, I would be able to bring her around to my way of thinking. This time I was fighting for everything I believed could be made to happen. Astrologically, to me it was so clear it was transparent.

I finally convinced her that despite the way Russian leaders used to be, Gorbachev was different. I warned her repeatedly that it would be disastrous for Ronnie to go to Geneva with mistaken preconceptions and his old outmoded bias.

"Ronnie's 'Evil Empire' attitude has to go before he can meet with Mikhail Gorbachev at Geneva," I told her. "Gorbachev's Aquarian planet is in such harmony with Ronnie's, you'll see," I said. "They'll share a vision. What's more, when Ronnie and Gorbachev meet, they'll get along famously, better than you can imagine if—and this is a very big if—Ronnie goes to Geneva with the proper attitude."

"I know you are right," Nancy said. "But it won't be easy to change Ronnie. First, I'll have to persuade him. You know as well as I do how he feels about Russian leaders. I'll have to make him realize what you say about Gorbachev is true."

"You will," I said.

I have never been more positive.

I remembered a true story told to me many years before by a man who had fought on the German side in World War I. After months in the trenches, the men were miserable with lice and suffering from dysentery. In such a war, I remember his telling me, you fought to keep yourself alive and out of enemy fire. Unless you were foolhardy, you never went in for heroics. Just as you didn't volunteer when someone was needed to peel potatoes.

It was Christmas Eve and very cold. Suddenly, as if by mutual consent, the shooting stopped at nightfall, although there had been no formal cease-fire. Despite the lice and the filth and all the other discomforts on both sides, men rested, in some cases for the first time since they entered the trenches. There were a few random instances of gunfire during the night, but mostly it was silent.

The next day, Christmas Day, the fighting resumed. But the German told me he noticed something extraordinary. At the edge of the trench at dawn he found some chocolate bars and several packages of cigarettes one lone British soldier must have hoarded for months for a treat to celebrate his Christmas. This British soldier crossed over no man's land and risked his life to deliver his Christmas offering to an enemy he'd never met.

There weren't many people who felt that way so long ago. But as long as there was even one, there was the possibility that the spirit of peace that begins with the individual could spread and extend to nations. Now everywhere people are longing for peace, believing it is possible.

I doubt that the Cain and Abel in human beings will ever be entirely eliminated. But in the potential chemistry between two of the world's most powerful men, if even one of them went forth with the proper attitude, I felt they could take up where the lone British soldier left off and accomplish miracles.

We'd been talking for hours. Both us of were tired. "I won't say another word," I told her. "You know how to handle Ronnie. I'll leave the way you go about doing it up to you!" I knew she was more than equal to her task.

"Sometimes," she told me, "he can be very stubborn." But I knew she was usually able to manage him for his own good or the good of the country.

## The Briefing for Geneva

As usual, Mrs. Reagan insisted on being consulted on the timing of every Presidential appearance and action so that she could consult her Friend in San Francisco about the astrological factor. The large number of details involved must have placed a heavy burden on the poor woman, who was called upon not only to choose auspicious moments for meetings between the two most powerful men on our planet, but also to draw up horoscopes that presumably provided clues to the character and probable behavior of Gorbachev.

—Donald Regan, *For the Record*

As I mentioned earlier, from the moment I calculated Mikhail Gorbachev's horoscope, placed it beside Ronald Reagan's and compared these two incredible charts, I knew that the chemistry between these two great leaders had breathtaking possibilities.

In that first session, I don't know how many times I repeated to Nancy that while Gorbachev was tough, he was also highly intelligent and open to new ideas, and that he had vision like Ronnie. I told her that together, these two great men, because of a shared humanitarian vision, could do something never before deemed possible in world history.

I briefed the President through Nancy for every meeting with Gorbachev in Geneva. I also tried to brief her for her teas alone with Raisa, which I knew in advance would not be harmonious; it looked like a non-take from the chart of the time and place they were first to meet at Maison Saussure, an 18th-century chateau on Lake Geneva owned by the Aga Khan.

Nancy did not ordinarily display the temperament of a prima donna. On the other hand, she was accustomed to occupying center stage. So was Raisa. In her own country, I learned Raisa was not overly popular. The consensus was that she dressed too well and was pretty autocratic. She had been as criticized in the Soviet Union for various forms of extravagance and sophisticated dressing as her American counterpart had been. And she too was accustomed to have the limelight shine directly on herself.

Nancy had gone to Geneva prepared to be friendly with the Soviet leader's wife. Nancy was accustomed to good manners, and she tried to make polite conversation. Raisa was anything but friendly or polite. So in a not overly civilized fashion, the two leaders' wives were fated to clash, just as their two husbands were destined to share a vision and get along.

My most penetrating insight regarding Ronnie's initial approach to Gorbachev couldn't have been simpler. It was as simple as Mother's insight about Mondale choosing Ferraro for his running mate. Common sense confirmed what I saw astrologically. Gorbachev had reached his high position because of the approval of powerful older men. Older men had given him his breaks. And it was because of older men admiring his precocious abilities and promoting him that he had had the ultimate chance to shine. Ronald Reagan was twenty years his senior. I felt that Gorbachev would be very comfortable dealing with the President at that stage of Gorbachev's career.

You must remember that the President had occupied a formidable position on the world stage for over five years. He was accepted and recognized globally. Gorbachev was making his debut, as it were, into a larger arena than the one he'd previously occupied. He was not unaware of the advantage of appearing in the same spotlight with Ronald Reagan. In addition to that, he would feel comfortable being shown the ropes, as it were, by an older man.

This first time they were not really meeting as equals. Ronnie was a recognized world figure. Despite his formidable backing and credentials, Gorbachev was a newcomer. I felt that if Ron-

I was responsible for timing all Presidential press conferences. In this picture, on March 20, 1987, Reagan gives his first press conference since the beginning of the Irangate scandal in November of 1986. Despite intense pressure, I advised Reagan not to appear at unfavorable or dangerous times, because I saw terrifying configurations in his horoscope which indicated assassination or other threats to his safety. (AP/Wide World Photos)

Donald Regan has said that he wrote about astrology in his book because it was an essential truth about the way the Reagans operated. Regan cooperated with the instructions I gave through Nancy, but resented them in a way that Michael Deaver had not. (UPI/Bettmann Newsphotos)

Michael Deaver, the President's first chief of staff, was very good about seeing to it that what I wanted was done.

(UPI/Bettmann Newsphotos)

After Donald Regan's resignation, Howard Baker became chief of staff. He had no problem with astrology, and I was never told that he objected to anything Nancy and I had planned. Nancy told me that Baker's own father-in-law, long-time Senator Everett Dirksen, never made a move without first consulting an astrologer.

On April 19, 1985, concentration camp survivor Elie Wiesel implores the President to cancel his visit to the cemetery in Bitburg, Germany, which contains the graves of some of Hitler's storm troopers.   In center is then Vice President Bush. Wiesel's protests bothered Nancy, and she continually referred to him as "that man." (UPI/Bettmann Newsphotos)

Nancy asked me to time the President's visits to Bergen-Belsen, the concentration camp, and to Bitburg. I chose the (astrologically) highly visible time of 11:45 A.M. for Bergen-Belsen. For the visit to Bitburg, I chose 2:45 P.M., which would make it less controversial. Right, President Reagan lays a wreath at Bergen-Belsen. Below, he walks with West German Chancellor Helmut Kohl, West German General Johannes Steinhoff, and General Matthew B. Ridgeway at Bitburg military cemetery.

I chose the time of 10:00 A.M. on November 14, 1983, for Reagan's visit to the demilitarized zone between North and South Korea. My choice protected the President from possible dangers, and insured that the visit would be well publicized. Above, President Reagan, escorted by Lt. Gen. Charles Preysler, Commander of the U.S. Guard Post at the DMZ, views North Korean positions from the Post observation deck. (UPI/Bettmann Newsphotos)

I knew from my charts of the meeting in Reykjavik, Iceland, that a final resolution there would take longer than anyone had planned. The visit did last longer than expected, but both sides were disappointed by the way the visit turned out. Above, Reagan and Gorbachev say their farewells in Reykjavik on October 12, 1986, after their fourth and final session of talks.     (AP/Wide World Photos)

I knew from the moment I looked at these two leaders' charts that they were destined to communicate, exchange ideas, and to share a vision of the world. Despite the stall at Reykjavik, I knew that, together, they would improve the relationships between the superpowers. Above, Reagan and Gorbachev chat at a fireplace in the Villa Fleur d'Eau at Versoix near Geneva in November, 1985. (AP/Wide World Photos)

nie was friendly and welcomed him with his usual gracious and charming attitude, Gorbachev would respond. I knew that this, above all other occasions, was Ronnie's chance to meet the newly elected Soviet leader at his most impressionable and that Gorbachev would be more receptive to Ronnie's ideas and proposals than later, after he assumed an equal place in the global spotlight and became more solidly entrenched as a principal player on the world stage.

I told Nancy that Ronnie must also be wary throughout the Geneva meetings, to listen as well as to talk, and that Gorbachev would reveal a secret during their conversations, perhaps deliberately. According to his horoscope, Gorbachev was not given to inadvertently telling tales out of school, so I figured he would say deliberately whatever he wanted Ronnie to think he'd just let slip.

It was a situation made to order for Ronnie. He had the military might, the missiles in Europe, a strong economy at home, and above all, SDI, the Strategic Defense Initiative, popularly known as "Star Wars." He'd done everything to prepare himself for the meeting with the new Russian leader.

"Ronnie has the perfect setup," I said to Nancy.

I knew from Gorbachev's chart (I believe this was known at the time, but the astrology confirmed it also) that Gorbachev's worst problems were economic. "It only makes sense," I said, "for both sides to agree to reduce the grandiose military expenditures that are causing the national debt to rise in the U.S.A. and the Soviets to have an abysmal standard of living." I added, "Ronnie will be able to reason with Gorbachev and convince him of doing things our way. You know—freedom and free enterprise."

I'm sure I wasn't the only one on the Reagan team who knew about Gorbachev's internal economic disaster, that unilateral disarmament was as advantageous for him as it was for us. What I knew about this from analyzing Gorbachev's horoscope, the rest of them knew from experts' reports. Gorbachev himself had to be painfully aware of this.

I suggested to Nancy that the way to begin the Geneva talks was by being friendly, that Ronnie's consummate charm could be used constructively to convince an open-minded, modern, highly intelligent Gorbachev to accept ideas heretofore unacceptable ideologically but now of practical value in the Soviet Union.

Through Nancy, I had to prepare the President for his first meeting with the new Soviet leader. Gorbachev had the power to make far-reaching changes on many levels. It was not only for his own country's sake, but for the entire world that Ronnie perform the mission he had been sent to do, to take the first step toward reconciliation with the Soviets and, yes, toward effecting change in the U.S.S.R.

I convinced Nancy that the chemistry between these two most powerful men not only could change Russia and the relations between the superpowers but could alter the course of world history.

"Ronnie should go to Geneva," I said, "cautious, of course, playing his cards close to the chest, yes, but not as a sworn antagonist, rather as a potential peacemaker and friend."

Further, I told Nancy that it was essential that Ronnie's attitude be conciliatory, not confrontational. "Ronnie has an incomparable chance to persuade Gorbachev to do things our way!"

"Do me a favor," I told Nancy. "Ronnie can be so charming and persuasive. Get him to exercise his supersalemanship ability on Gorbachev. Get him to sell arms reduction, democracy, human rights and free enterprise to the Secretary General. If he goes to Geneva with the right attitude, he can accomplish miracles!"

## The Time of the Departure of Air Force One
## for Geneva

As I've said previously, sometimes an astrologer can find a perfect time to begin a journey. A time that insures success and eliminates troubles. What one wishes to happen will happen. The moment must exist already in the flow of time before an astrologer can extract it and make use of it. When something is meant to be, the time that describes the event is already there, like bonbons in a candy store. You have only to select one.

November 16, 1985, at 8:35 A.M. was the time I chose for Air Force One to depart for Geneva. What I wanted most was for Gorbachev to be willing to listen to what Ronnie had to say, and hopefully to be persuaded to come over to his way of thinking. I did this in a classic way, astrologically, by putting the planet that represented Ronnie's Russian counterpart, i.e., Gorbachev, in the First house, or the Ascendant, of the chart, so that he would naturally be drawn to Ronnie. This chart, coupled with the chemistry shown between the two leaders' charts, enclosed the meeting I visualized like the frame of a beautiful painting.

The Summit took place on November 19–21, and although it did not produce an accord on arms control or other major issues, it did help put U.S.-Soviet relations back on a business-like basis and stripped the confrontational rhetoric.

This was Ronald Reagan's first impression of Gorbachev at Geneva. Doris Klein Bacon, in an interview of Ronald Reagan, quotes the President:

He was certainly very different. The first day at Geneva I suggested that he and I go out and get some fresh air and have a little meeting alone. Before I had the sentence finished, he was out of his chair. [At the beach cottage by the lake] I told him, "This is a unique situation. Here we are. Two men in a room together. We're the only two in the world who could bring about World War III. At the same time, maybe we're the only two who could bring about world peace." I suggested that it would be a good thing if maybe we could get together and eliminate the causes of [our mutual] mistrust. And he seemed to nod in agreement on that.

And *U.S. News & World Report*, in its January 13, 1986, issue has the following caption beneath a picture of several TV screens and a crowd assembled:

MESSAGE FROM MIKHAIL. . . . Shoppers in Philadelphia pause to watch an unfamiliar New Year's Day greeting from Soviet leader Mikhail Gorbachev wishing every American family "good health, peace and happiness." If Gorbachev's soft words—sandwiched between parades and football bowls—bemused Americans, Soviet citizens were more startled when President Reagan, flanked by the U.S. flag, a portrait of First Lady Nancy and a potted poinsettia, turned up without notice on Moscow TV news and called on them to help make 1986 "a year of peace."

# XIV

# Reykjavik

On September 18, 1986, the dearest person I have ever known left this life. We both knew when it was to be. She and I had shared philosophical beliefs concerning death, and we had discussed it. Her last breath was gentle as her life had been. She was a rare individual—intelligent, just, generous and kind. Her sensitivity to others' feelings was exquisite. I will never cease to miss her.

The morning after Mother died, Nancy called me very early. I said, "Nancy, my mother died yesterday. Call back some other time. I don't feel like talking."

"But Joan," she insisted, "this is important! I can't wait. You must look at something now. It's vitally important."

I mumbled something incoherent. Normally, I was there for her, but that morning the last person I felt like talking to was Nancy.

"Joan," she persisted, "Ronnie and I are the only two people in the country who know this. You will be the third person."

147

"Well?" I said.

"This morning Gorbachev proposed that Ronnie go to a secret meeting with him in Reykjavik. My question is, Should Ronnie go? And will the meeting be kept secret?"

"Where on earth is Reykjavik and how do you spell it?"

"It's in Iceland." She spelled it out for me.

"Call back in an hour," I said. "By then, I'll have the answer."

The invitation from Gorbachev came at a time when relations between the Soviet Union and the United States were virtually at a standstill. The KGB had arrested Nicholas Daniloff, the Moscow correspondent for *U.S. News & World Report*, on trumped-up charges after Gennadi Zakharov, a KGB agent using his United Nations employment as cover, was arrested by the FBI in New York and charged with espionage. The Soviet's ploy was obviously to exchange an innocent American for a guilty Russian.

According to Donald Regan's account in *For the Record*, President Reagan had been upbraiding Soviet Foreign Minister Eduard Shevardnadze in the Oval Office over the incident. The Foreign Minister had come to deliver a letter, which the President left unopened and unread until the forty-five minute lecture he gave the Foreign Minister had ended and Shevardnadze had departed.

In *For the Record*, Donald Regan wrote:

> Gorbachev did not mention the Daniloff case. Instead he proposed that he and Reagan meet as soon as possible to discuss the complete elimination of Soviet and U.S. intermediate-range nuclear missiles from Europe, without taking into account French and British missiles.

The way the message had been delivered is clear to me now. Whether or not Nancy stretched the truth when she told me I was the third person to know about the proposal, I do not know.

I only know what she said on the phone the morning after my mother died. I remember every word she said exactly as I have written it.

This was the first signal of a possible breakthrough in the arms agreement. I understood quite well what Reykjavik might mean for the hopeful millions who had so often seen their dreams of peace vanish like a mirage as they approached it. For the moment, I put my personal grief aside and turned my attention to Ronald Reagan's horoscope.

I have a method of determining the best place for an individual to be during a given time period. I also study certain sensitive charts which helped me with the in-depth work I did routinely for the Reagans. These charts were always calculated for Washington by the able young astrologer who does my computer work. Nicki never suspected that I was doing the Reagan's astrology until almost the very end, because I did the calculations by hand when the Washington charts needed to be transposed to other places.

After casting up Ronnie's location chart for the proposed Reykjavik visit, I compared it with this chart for Washington during the same period. The Washington chart was mediocre to poor. The Reykjavik chart was stupendous. There was no question that Ronnie should go to Reykjavik for his second historic meeting with Gorbachev.

When Nancy called back, I told her, "Not only should Ronnie go, he will go."

"Will the meeting be kept secret?" Nancy asked.

"No," I said, "the whole world will know. There is no chance of its being secret."

I explained to her the difference between the two charts. The one described Ronnie living life as usual in Washington as inconspicuously as is possible for a president. The other was one of the most visible charts I've ever encountered. Every planet was prominently placed in the upper half of the horoscope circle. There was no question in my mind that the meeting would take place and that it would attract global attention.

Later, Nancy asked me to choose a departure time for Air Force One to leave for Reykjavik. It was an excellent chart. It promised favorable results from the upcoming summit.

The State Department, the Secretary of State and the President agreed with the Russians on scheduled meeting times before every summit. The media have asked me again and again whether I determined these important meeting times astrologically. I have repeatedly denied doing so. Quite emphatically, I didn't choose them.

However, Nancy always gave me a list of summit meeting times and I gave her my analysis of each of them, with caveats and suggestions. I have every reason to believe that these proved very helpful.

I examined carefully the chart of the first meeting of these two great leaders face to face since the Geneva Summit. I was able to find an excellent time for the President's departure for Reykjavik. A chart of the moment Air Force One took off from Andrews Air Force Base described what would happen during that trip, whether its purpose would be realized or not and indicated its physical safety.

But the first meeting time in Reykjavik, which determined the course of the conference, was not as promising. It suggested to me that a final resolution of the talks would take longer than anyone then planned, perhaps months, perhaps a year or more. The one thing I knew for certain from both charts was that there would be a delay.

Encouraged by what I saw in the departure chart, I told Nancy to tell Ronnie and Shultz to lengthen the meeting times and even to stay over later than planned, hoping that by extending them, the last meetings would be successful. However, I told Nancy that if they were not, Reykjavik should be regarded as a step along the way and that any efforts made there would not be wasted in the long view. While Reagan was criticized for taking so short a time to prepare for the summit, it is now evident that my analysis was correct. What was accomplished at Reykjavik was seminal.

According to Regan, Reagan and Gorbachev spent nine hours and forty-eight minutes in negotiation. It was a tiring ordeal. Both leaders were close to exhaustion.

Nancy called the weekend the summit was in progress. I told her to tell Ronnie and Shultz to keep trying until the last minute of the visit. As it was, they stayed later than planned and were disappointed by the way the visit turned out. But I told Nancy to tell them not to worry, that good was sure to come out of it eventually.

I happen to know that the final meeting that took place— which according to Regan, occurred between 5:32 and 6:30 on Sunday night—was originally unscheduled. Regan's account of that meeting is exciting.

As was later reported, the two leaders made progress on regional, bilateral, and human rights issues. They also agreed in principle to the Soviet proposal for a reduction in intermediate missiles to zero in Europe, 100 in Asia, and 100 in the United States. They were for eliminating strategic nuclear weapons in two five-year periods while research, testing, and development of SDI continued. Nothing was said about confining such development to the laboratory, as Gorbachev had originally proposed in his letter to Reagan.

What, Reagan asked Gorbachev, had he meant by the reference in his letter to "the elimination of all strategic forces"?

"I meant I would favor eliminating all nuclear weapons," Gorbachev replied.

*All* nuclear weapons? Reagan said. Well, Mikhail, that's

exactly what I've been talking about all along. That's what we have long wanted to do—get rid of all nuclear weapons. That's always been my goal.

"Then why don't we agree on it?" Gorbachev asked.

We should, Reagan said. That's what I've been trying to tell you.

It was a historic moment. The two leaders had brought the world to one of its great turning points. Both understood this very clearly.

Then came the impasse. Mikhail Gorbachev said, "I agree. But this must be done in conjunction with a ten-year extension of the ABM treaty and a ban on the development and testing of SDI outside the laboratory."

*Outside the laboratory.* Those words negated all that had been agreed upon. As soon as they were uttered, Reagan and Gorbachev were down from the mountaintop and right back where they had started.

Reagan, astonished by this sudden reversal, said, Absolutely not. I am willing to discuss all details, including the timing, of a plan to eliminate all nuclear weapons in conjunction with a plan to reduce conventional forces to a state of balance. But I will not discuss anything that gives you the upper hand by eliminating SDI.

Gorbachev did not reply. After a long silence, Reagan assumed that the Soviet leader had nothing more to say. Thereupon he closed his briefing book and stood up. Gorbachev seemed startled by the President's action and remained in his chair for a moment in puzzlement. Then he rose to his feet also. The summit at Reykjavik was over.

—Donald Regan, *For the Record*

The Monday after he returned from Reykjavik, President Reagan delivered a television speech explaining what had happened. It wasn't a triumphant return, but he made the best of it.

It would have been politically expedient for him to make an unsound agreement at the time and to return to Washington in apparent triumph. But his stance was sound, his integrity unassailable.

In the beginning, the Reykjavik meeting was to include only men; Nancy hadn't planned on going. Very late in the planning stages, Nancy learned that Raisa would accompany her husband. Nancy felt, I think, that Raisa had invited herself deliberately to show off. Nancy decided not to go, that wives would be superfluous. I think it was a wise decision. Nonetheless, Nancy was irked by Raisa's rather obvious attempt to upstage her American counterpart.

I never had even a hint about Raisa's date and place of birth. It would have interested me to have been able to compare her chart with Nancy's. But neither needed astrology to know that they didn't get along. It was evident at that first stiff, unfriendly tea in Geneva. Still, it was better that their husbands got along than that they did. From what Nancy said, it was easier for her to relate to Gorbachev. That may have been part of the reason for Raisa's attitude. According to Nancy, Raisa was a doctrinaire communist and hard-liner, and she may have resented her husband's more liberal approach to capitalists.

# XV

# Irangate

It is awesome to be an astrologer. I will never stop being amazed at what an astrologer can do. With only the time and place of birth to go on, an astrologer can describe the character an individual was born with, the kind of person he will develop into and the experiences he will have during his life. An astrologer can also assess the nature of the external forces that will aid or hinder him.

The average person's horoscope is not so well put together. But the horoscopes of great men and women are always organized purposefully. Some great leaders spend their energies on conquest. Others devote their lives to a noble cause. An enlightened astrologer can help a great leader to harness the cosmic forces to his purposes, but only for a time.

Napoleon spent his final years on St. Helena. Lincoln and Gandhi were murdered by assassins. Roosevelt died in office. Churchill lived to old age, but death claimed him before he could finish his memoirs. Nixon was defeated at the height of his career, but he lives on. No one masters the cosmic forces forever. Sooner or later they turn against us, if only at the end.

In early November, 1986, an account in *Al Shiraa*, an obscure Iranian magazine, revealed that Robert McFarlane had flown into Tehran on a secret mission to sell U.S. weapons to Khomeini's government. The *Washington Post* and the *Los Angeles Times* caught wind of this. When Attorney General Edwin Meese discovered that the proceeds from the sale had been diverted to the Contras, the Irangate scandal came out into the open and the President was blamed. Nancy asked me if it was serious and how long it would last. I told her the Administration chart had indicated scandal, a hospital experience for the President as well as the danger of assassination.

I was in no way involved in the nitty gritty of Irangate. But I did predict it in a roundabout way. I had seen from the Administration chart that there was the possibility of scandal. But what really alarmed me was what I also saw unequivocally: the danger of assassination. This affected my advice to Nancy regarding the President's public exposure after the Irangate scandal broke.

In the fall of 1986, the most sensitive indicator I applied to the President's chart showed that he would be very much in the limelight. It was unusual, even with the chart of someone of his great prominence, to see such high visibility week after week. What I saw was the beginning of Irangate.

The first advice I gave Nancy on handling the Irangate mess was based on textbook American history. I said that the President ought to assert himself and tell Congress that the Constitution gave him the right to deal with foreign affairs, that the Boland Amendment was unconstitutional because it limited the President's powers in this type of situation. I remembered that James Madison had said that the real danger to the Republic he had set up in the Constitution would be the "interference with the Executive by Congress." He felt, and quite rightly, that this was the only major defect in the original Constitution. After two centuries, the danger Madison foresaw had materialized.

Theoretically, with Madison in mind, I would have agreed with Donald Regan that the President should fight, should go on the road immediately and defend his position and policies. In the beginning, that was my own gut reaction. However, when I studied the President's horoscope for the months between December of 1986 and August of 1987, that reaction struck me as not only foolhardy but downright reckless.

Horrendous configurations began to affect Ronald Reagan's chart in early November. I didn't doubt for one moment that from that time on, for a number of months, the President needed the utmost physical protection.

From February through May 1987 the indications were terrifying. When I saw them coming, I was fearful that even astrology would not be able to protect him. As I have said, an enlightened astrologer can help a great leader to harness the cosmic forces to his purposes but only for a time. The time had come when I would not be able completely to avoid dangers to the President. It was fated and unavoidable.

No human being can prevail when the malevolent movements of Uranus and Saturn go against his horoscope. Uranus disrupts a life suddenly and unexpectedly. It was a prolonged two-year configuration of Uranus to the most sensitive degree in Nixon's horoscope that caused Watergate and his eventual resignation from the presidency. At its worst, Uranus is a throne-toppler.

Saturn is a stern disciplinarian, who gives us our hardest lessons. It is the most discouraging planet. There is no way to avoid Saturn's ill effects. By itself, Saturn is set in cement. When Saturn combines with the explosive, upsetting Uranus to relate unfavorably to an individual's horoscope, it is bound to be destabilizing, demoralizing and depressing. In astrology, a double configuration such as this can be responsible for any number of different repercussions. It can even result in the afflicted individual's death.

The moving Uranus on the President's Ascendant or Rising Sign signaled the surprise announcement Meese made. In February of 1987, when Saturn moved to the place first occupied by the moving Uranus, Nancy told me it was the first time since they had met that Ronnie had been anything but optimistic. This is typical of Saturn's action. These two planets were in Sagittarius, the sign that has so much to do with foreigners and foreign affairs and legal and judicial matters.

In Ronald Reagan's case during Irangate and after, these two evil planets turning against him in the most personal area of his chart were bound to upset and depress him, and weakened him physically by a second cancer operation in January of 1987. Viewing the chart of this time period was rather like seeing the elemental force of a tornado coming in the distance. In that situation, sensible people run to their storm cellar and fasten the top down tightly. At such a time, the farmer would hardly try to protect his carefully planted crops. His immediate reaction would be to seek shelter.

I have been criticized by Regan and others for severely limiting the President's exposure to the media and the public during this period between his second operation for cancer and the increasing furor over Irangate. The media was crying out for press conferences, which in my opinion would have been disastrous to the President's interests and during which he would have been at a disadvantage, unable to fend off the shower of criticism which was to be expected but which he would not have had his usual ability to combat.

Nancy told me, "Donald Regan expects Ronnie to go on the road to defend his policies a week after his second operation for cancer."

"I fear not only for Ronnie's health, I fear for his physical safety now," I told her. "The malevolence of both Saturn and Uranus turning against him could cost him his life."

"I don't care what anyone says," Nancy said. "I won't have Ronnie go on the road a week out of the hospital."

I reinforced her feelings one hundred percent, and later she reinforced me.

I can remember telling her, "I don't want him to have a press conference now. I don't see a decent time for almost three months."

Nancy replied, "Regan is pressing me to have him defend his policies in strategic places in different parts of the country."

I said, "No, he can't do it now. Not only will no one respond to his reasoning. His life is in danger and I am not referring to health. There is danger of impeachment during this period, and the danger of assassination is very real," I kept insisting.

Nancy listened to me, and while we have both been criticized, I am convinced that I was absolutely correct in the advice I gave her and she in following it.

I had before me during that period a dread example, an awful warning in the person of a 45-year-old Vietnamese man who worked for us one or two days a week. I always did the horoscopes of the people who came into our apartment so that I would know whether it was safe to have them around and also so that I could warn them if I saw danger in their horoscopes.

Le Hai was a dapper little man, who wanted nothing more than to do his job and go dancing on the weekends with his new wife. He did good work, and he enjoyed life. He happened to know the time of his birth to the minute. I had an accurate chart.

The same terrible movements that were affecting the President were affecting Le Hai. A week before danger was due, I warned Le Hai to be careful. I was fearful because he had a job delivering newspapers in the dark hours of early morning. Two days after I first warned him, he came to work, his thin face swollen round. He had been severely beaten by a dope addict on the street.

Quite typically, these malevolent moving planets go back and forth, on and off a crucial degree in a person's horoscope. The next time I warned Le Hai, I was very sad to learn that his wife gave birth to the infant girl they had wanted so desperately. The baby was defective; she died within two days.

I was afraid for Le Hai the last time these moving planets were due to affect him. But I hoped a warning would help. He had recently told me that he had been to a Vietnamese astrologer who told him he was entering one of the best years of his life. I shook my head and told him, "I don't think so. You must be very careful right now." I warned him on Wednesday, then again on Thursday.

Friday morning, he didn't come to work. My sister said, "I am sure something terrible has happened to Le Hai or he would have called."

Later that day, we learned that Le Hai had been struck by a bread truck that went through a red light. He was hit in the head and never regained consciousness. The day after the accident, Le Hai died.

I have seen this type of movement by malevolent planets cause every kind of ill from psychological or bodily damage to trouble to loved ones to actual physical death. You can understand why, when I saw similar configurations affecting the President's horoscope, that I was afraid. I couldn't protect Le Hai. He had to walk on the street, drive a car and do his early morning job.

But I could protect the President. I have never been so determined or so sure of myself. Nancy listened to me. We reinforced each other. I have the utmost respect for the virulence of Saturn and Uranus when they combine to go against a person's chart.

Reagan's troubles during Irangate were absolutely fated.

There was no way to contend with them actively without his being utterly destroyed, both politically and physically. When the cosmic forces turn against one, it is best to run for cover and, insofar as is possible, to conceal oneself until their fury abates.

I have seen example after example throughout my years of studying and practicing astrology, and I know whereof I speak. But I had the sad example of Le Hai, whom I couldn't protect, during the same period. I was utterly determined to protect the President. I apologize to no one. Because Nancy believed in what I told her, the President survived his second term.

### Regan's Resignation

About two months after Nancy and I agreed that the President should not go on the road in opposition to Donald Regan's wishes, the President's Chief of Staff was given no choice but to resign. Nancy felt, I supposed rightly, that Donald Regan, who had been an excellent Secretary of the Treasury, was not suited temperamentally to be Chief of Staff. She told me she was determined to replace him. From what I gathered, they were at swords' points. She felt he had mismanaged the Iran-Contra affair, and was furious that he wanted the President to go on the road to defend his policies a week after his second operation for cancer. As his wife, she had every right to feel this way and to protect her husband.

It wasn't so much what she did; it was the way she went about it. She behaved very ill-advisedly and misjudged the repercussions incumbent in not only removing but deliberately and unnecessarily disgracing a man who did not deserve such treatment. The Greeks had a word for her kind of action: hubris, or arrogance. Every Greek tragedy dramatizes the crisis of a noble character whose hubris, or arrogance, precedes his downfall. In other words, one should not let either royal ancestry or the exercise of great power go to one's head!

I doubt that Nancy was acquainted either with Euripides or with Aeschylus, but she would have done well to take heed of the classic warning, at that time no doubt unknown to her. I was afraid for her when she exulted to me the day she got rid of Regan that the press corps and staff at the White House had clapped when he left the premises for the final time.

She didn't have to go about it that way. After all, Regan had served the administration brilliantly and honorably before he changed jobs with James Baker, Jr. From the reports, he himself was as autocratic as Nancy. The absolutely essential characteristic a Chief of Staff must offer is a diplomatic approach to people and problems. An autocrat is not suited to the post, but removing such a man must be handled cautiously and with the softest of velvet gloves.

Donald Regan had served honorably both as Secretary of the Treasury and as Chief of Staff, both very important positions, and he did not deserve the public humiliation of being dismissed with a lack of consideration that was motivated by malice and the desire for revenge.

Nancy felt justified in this ill-considered behavior. I don't suppose to this day she is aware of what was wrong with it. But Regan took his own revenge, and if I hadn't been very careful in handling the matter the way I did when the news broke about my being the Reagans' astrologer, it could have done damage to the party in the 1988 elections. But I am glad that didn't happen.

As Nancy grew stronger, Ronnie weakened. Nancy started out as a partner who complemented and helped her husband by being aware of the people surrounding him, their motives and loyalty. Then she became an equal partner, and after that, the dominant force.

As was typical of many women born in the Twenties, Nancy felt that the accepted way for a woman to express herself was through her husband. Although she'd had a brief career as an actress, to her it didn't really count. What mattered to her was having a home of her own, babies and a husband she backed with her considerable resourcefulness.

Once I had succeeded in reforming her image, she basked in the glow for a time. Then further ambition took over. She realized that she was a power in her own right. She devoted herself tirelessly to promoting her own interests as she had heretofore promoted her husband's. Gradually, her desire to back Ronnie from behind the scenes diminished. She wished to be a political power openly.

In the beginning, she had had a sixth sense about the people around the President, and she was ruthless in eliminating people she felt weren't serving him well or who had outlived their usefulness. She was clever about manipulating people and situations and was never restrained by sentiment or consideration of the feelings and needs of others.

She knew John Sears was not the right campaign director. She knew she needed the drama of a debate in the last days of the campaign in 1980. When Ronnie became President, she stopped looking at him doe-eyed during his speeches, as she had done when he was Governor, but she continued supporting him without publicly intruding herself.

When she began to reap the honors that for a time were showered on her, her strongest motivating factor was her place in history right alongside her husband, as a dominant and powerful political force in her own right.

I remember my father saying that after a while all presidents are isolated dangerously. People in awe of high office defer to them; few people ever contradict them or tell them the truth. Lack of perspective is an occupational hazard of the presidency, as is the feeling that you, the President, can do no wrong.

This is an excerpt from a letter I wrote Nancy concerning presidential loss of perspective:

> To wield great power is very much like being super rich. The rich man like the man of power can have in his immediate circle sycophants who please him because they always say "yes," while at the same time, they can be deceitful and disloyal behind his back. Or maybe they are weak characters afraid to offend the great man by disagreeing. The man who wields power begins to believe that he is invincible and infallible. It is hard in this atmosphere of "you can do no wrong" to preserve that touch of humility that characterizes the truly great. Nothing is more dangerous than this isolation at the top. It has always been the Achilles heel of powerful men and wealthy men. The truly great man is his own man and knows how to listen to those who have proven they have his best interests at heart.

In the early days, Ronnie would be stubborn sometimes when Nancy would tell him things for his own good that no one else dared to say to him. However, it was Nancy, not the President, who fell prey to the idea that she could do no wrong.

Following Donald Regan's resignation, Howard Baker was appointed Chief of Staff on February 27, 1987. He was more to Nancy's liking. But I always felt that in an entirely different way, he was as wrong for the job as Donald Regan had been. As far as Nancy's using astrology, Howard Baker was more sympathetic than Regan. Nancy told me that Howard Baker's own father-in-law, the highly respected, long-time Senator, Everett Dirksen, never made a move without first consulting his astrologer.

Howard Baker's main deficiency, as I saw it, was the same as Regan's. Both men were better suited to their previous positions. Howard Baker had served with great distinction in Congress for many years. To serve as the Majority Leader of the

Senate, one must be a master of compromise. That is how solutions are arrived at in legislative bodies. But it is not the best preparation or experience for a Chief of Staff at the White House.

On February 3, 1988, the President's Contra Aid Package was defeated in the House by eight votes. After that, Howard Baker, in league with Nancy, engineered the compromise with Speaker of the House Jim Wright regarding Nicaragua. At that time, Wright had not been discredited and forced to resign. Wright wanted the Nicaragua Peace Plan for political reasons, and through his plan, Ortega gained time and military strength. Ortega was no doubt laughing up his sleeve at our credulity. From our standpoint, the compromise was not only injudicious, it was unrealistic.

At that point, Ronald Reagan, against his best judgment, was forced into a corner he could never have been in two years earlier. But he didn't believe in the compromise then or ever. I could see in his expression on television when he had to appear to agree with it, "You'll have to learn the hard way. My hands are tied." He didn't actually say it, but it was written all over his face.

President Reagan reasoned that if the Sandinistas spread communism throughout Central America, their forces would have a stranglehold on the neck dividing the continents, isolating North America from the rest of the hemisphere. While Reagan's plan to aid the Contras fell into the hands of the wrong people and aiding the Contras was unpopular in many circles, history will one day prove that President Reagan was strategically correct.

Reagan is not alone historically in having a vision that people scoffed at, that met with resistance in Congress. In 1867, the United States was recovering from the Civil War and was embroiled in impeaching President Johnson, who, like Secretary of State William Seward and half a dozen Senators who shared the same vision, wanted to acquire Alaska from the Russians for $7,200,000. They were severely ridiculed both by Congress and the public. Alaska was nicknamed "Seward's Folly" or "Seward's Icebox," and the conventional wisdom was that nothing existed there but Eskimos and polar bears.

Seward finally got the purchase approved by the Senate by a margin of just one vote. The House of Representatives refused to appropriate the money until a questionable half-Austrian, half-Italian (who paraded as a Russian nobleman and married a wealthy American woman, having disposed of $125,000 he couldn't account for) managed to get the House to appropriate the funds for the purchase and then mysteriously disappeared.

Alaska's riches in oil and minerals, not to mention furs and fish and the pipeline, vindicate both President Johnson and William Seward. The whole purchase, amounting to less than two cents an acre for land of such great value, vindicates the vision of those few determined men.

Nancy and Howard Baker and Jim Wright had their compromise. It hasn't taken long to show how ill-advised the then politically expedient compromise was. Ortega's forces even now are expanding into El Salvador.

But malevolent planets had turned against Reagan, and there was no way for him to prevail. He might as well have been handcuffed on either side to his planetary jailers. Pluto, involved in the configuration of planets opposing him, provided the gag. Special interest groups combined with the media (this is typical of Pluto) to deny the President a voice. Before the February 3, 1988 vote giving aid to the Contras, none of the networks gave Ronald Reagan a chance to appeal to the American people. They denied air time to the President of the United States, who had been elected with an overwhelming mandate from the people. The reason they gave was that the speech was partisan and political. He was powerless and had to give in.

In January of 1987, I must say I concurred with Nancy regarding the protection of the President, but not in regard to Donald Regan. I never had Regan's horoscope nor did I have any part in what happened to him. But from the standpoint of astrology, I knew that it was unwise to expose the President to the public and the media during that period except at the very few safe times.

Donald Regan lists in *For the Record* the dates I ruled out in early 1987. I stand by everything I advised. There was a chance of impeachment and, as I mentioned previously, an even more terrifying danger of assassination. I would as soon have seen the President dive into water swarming with piranhas as expose him to the media and the public indiscriminately at that particular time.

Nancy heeded my warning. We reinforced one another. The President knew about it, and midway through the worst of Irangate she told me he asked her, "What does Joan say?" about when it would end. I told her to tell him the worst would be over in the investigations held during his presidency in early August of 1987, and so it was.

During that terrible period, Nancy told me that the President spent all his time glued to his television, listening to everything being said about Irangate, and that in contrast to his usual exuberant optimism, he was downcast, discouraged and depressed.

As is usual, when something is absolutely fated and there is nothing to do but to try to live through it, I provided Nancy with a way to comfort the President. I suggested to her that she give Ronnie some biographies of Lincoln. I told her what Lincoln had suffered during the last years of his presidency and that to put his troubles in perspective, Ronnie should read about Lincoln's terrible trials.

After the Tower Committee Report was finished, with its harmless admonitions, Irangate died down in early August, exactly when I said it would. At that time, I felt it was appropriate to write the President a letter. This letter concerned the subject of peace, as had the verbal message I'd delivered in the receiving line at the State Dinner.

I began, "Dear Ronnie." I felt it would be pretentious and hypocritical to address him as "Mr. President" when I knew him through his horoscope so well. When Nancy and I spoke of him during our phone calls, she always called him Ronnie. Once in a while, I referred to him as "the President," but most of the time, I called him "Ronnie" too.

Very often, Nancy would turn from the phone, when she was mid-conversation with me, to say something to him and would say, "I'm talking to Joan."

This is the letter I wrote to President Ronald Reagan, August 2, 1987.

Dear Ronnie,

With the exception of Washington, America's most outstanding presidents have been Aquarians. Lincoln, Roosevelt and Reagan. They occupy a very special place in their people's hearts but they have had their problems as well. It is said, "A great man, great problems."

It is also said that the only lasting evil a bad experience can do to anyone is to warp their judgment. This has not happened to you. You have borne up nobly during a period when your astrological transits could be likened to the adverse weather conditions that threaten to destroy a farmer's carefully planted crops. But you, the farmer unaltered by adversity, will come through your trials intact, and mindful of the rich harvests of past years, will surpass past successes. . . .

You have remained firm and balanced as your personal good aspects indicate and have gone about your business with a smile and now, having passed the test by so doing, you will emerge triumphant.

Already you have in place three brilliant strategies: the missiles in Europe, the development of SDI and the strong military.

It is my conviction that of the American presidents, Lincoln and Reagan will go down in world history as the very greatest. Both have Jupiter rulers. Lincoln's in Pisces, gave him the problem of slavery. Your ruler in Scorpio gave you the problem of war. And as Lincoln abolished slavery, you, Ronald Reagan, will bring peace to the world. Your vision will be vindicated, your role in history unparalleled.

As your astrologer, your steadfastness and courage, your true spiritual strength did not surprise me. They are only what I expected.

With admiration,
Joan

I sent the letter to Nancy with her code number on the envelope, as I always did to insure its reaching her, and she promised to deliver it to him. She called the minute he had read it, and he got on the phone and thanked me. He told me he was grateful for my encouragement in the letter and all I had done for the administration. At the end of our conversation, he said his usual, "God bless you." And I said, "God bless you," too.

# XVI

# Judges for the Supreme Court

From the President's chart and the mundane material for Washington, D.C., I thought that September of 1987 would be a nightmare. And so it was. The Bork hearings were a disaster as far as Reagan was concerned.

Nancy had not asked me to look at Bork's horoscope until after the fact. He had been proposed much earlier in the year, and I had not been consulted at that time regarding his chances. When I did, in fact, see his horoscope, I knew that the situation was hopeless. The same two planets that had been so hard on Ronnie during Irangate were again united, this time against Bork's chart, and I saw no chances for him at all. These malefic planets continued to afflict him for a year after the hearings ended.

The opposition to Bork had postponed the hearings while his

enemies gathered their forces to defeat him. In addition, at the time of the hearings, Bork was destined to be beaten. His chart, the mundane material for Washington, the July 4th, 1776, chart of the U.S.A.—all confirmed this.

Whether or not one agrees with his viewpoints, it was terrible to see a distinguished and brilliant jurist, revered by so many honorable, able colleagues, judged by his legal inferiors in a lynch mob atmosphere. Joseph Biden, Teddy Kennedy and Robert Byrd ganged up on him during the hearings. Appallingly, this great authority on law was being examined by certain people, some of whom had barely been able to pass their bar exams. However, if I had been consulted before he was proposed, I could have spared him the ordeal.

I didn't have a chart for the next nominee, Douglas Ginsberg. He withdrew because his wife had been involved in performing an abortion when in medical school, and it was discovered that he had smoked marijuana when a student and later when a member of the Harvard faculty. But before Anthony Kennedy was proposed, they called me in as the astrological problem solver. Nancy gave me Kennedy's date and place of birth and his mother's maiden name. This is all you need in California to get a photostat copy of someone's birth certificate. Normally, this contains the birthtime.

I knew, of course, from his horoscope that Kennedy would be confirmed, but the mood on Capitol Hill was not favorable for any nominee to the Supreme Court proposed by Reagan. Nancy felt it was wise to have me pick the time of the announcement.

When I was asked, it wasn't easy to find the right moment. But I have an astrological method (too technecal to explain) that enables me to choose a time when the indications are otherwise not promising but which nonetheless insures the success of a venture. This is something I can't always do, but on November 11th it was possible. Sometimes a few minutes or more either way do not affect the success of an undertaking. However, in this case, it was absolutely mandatory that this announcement be timed down to the second. The time was 11:32:25 A.M. exactly.

Nancy arranged to start a little early and stall until the person chosen to man the stopwatch gave the signal for the President to make the announcement. It was done with great care and absolute precision. With Kennedy, whose horoscope showed that he would be confirmed, everything had gone like clockwork. Literally! Anthony M. Kennedy was confirmed by a vote of 97-0 in the Senate on February 3, 1988.

Around that time, I read, or Nancy told me (I don't remember which), the date that Bush was planning to announce that he was running for President. I looked but didn't like the date the people planning the campaign had chosen. I suggested to Nancy a slightly earlier date that I liked better—a Monday instead of a Thursday in the same week, as I remember.

I have no idea whether or not Nancy got through to him, but he did announce he was running on the date I suggested. I didn't know where he was going to be nor did I select a time of day for him, so I can't claim any responsibility for what happened in November of '88. I'm glad he won, however. I think he is not only capable but a very decent man.

# XVII

# The Washington and Moscow Summits and the Signing of the INF Treaty

At the beginning of September 1987, Nancy told me that at long last there was a chance for the proposed Washington Summit. Reagan and Gorbachev had not met for almost a year, and the negotiations still continued. But we were both excited that an agreement on Intermediate-range Nuclear Forces might be reached before the end of the year, hopefully within a few months or earlier. When we began to plan, Nancy ruled out December because the calendar would be so full of other activities in the capital so close to the holidays.

I knew, at that time, that we hadn't yet succeeded in getting the terms we wanted. I also knew Ronnie was very anxious to finish what he had begun so brilliantly at Geneva and done so wisely at Reykjavik.

Ronnie had concluded the Iceland Summit just minutes away from a sweeping agreement because Gorbachev had sprung the surprise condition of limiting SDI to the laboratory. To Gorbachev's evident surprise, the President rose in the way any important executive does when he is dismissing someone and signaling the end of a conference. Ronnie could have had the appearance of a stunning victory had he compromised then.

At Reykjavik in October of 1986, he'd displayed perfect integrity and the utmost will power. A compromise would have been highly advantageous to him at the time. The quick fix was well within his reach. It would have made the sort of splash short-sighted men or lesser politicians would not have hesitated to make, to shore up their internal situation temporarily. But Reagan had been willing even to risk the appearance of defeat rather than agree to an expedient but unsound victory.

However, this time I was worried. Ronnie had about a year and a quarter to go before leaving the Oval Office. It would have been less than human not to want to wrap up all that he had planned and worked for and done so far. Here was a chance to tie up the package of two triumphant summits, first in Washington, then Moscow, with his own red, white and blue ribbon.

What American president at any time could boast of an achievement of this magnitude? In World Wars I and II, leaders, victorious in war, had made agreements that defeated enemies disarm. But never before in the history of the world had two great nations, each a formidable military power, disarmed unilaterally. The wish to achieve this heretofore undreamed of goal, especially after the near disgrace of Irangate, was even more desirable. The place in history this would assure the President was unparalleled.

You must remember that the Reagans were hobnobbing internationally with Queen Elizabeth II, whose position was assured for life, and Gorbachev, whose leadership in the U.S.S.R. was not determined by a Constitutional Amendment limiting him to two four-year terms, as is the case for an American president. Ronnie had relatively little time to achieve an ultimate and unparalleled place in history. Cutting corners was hard to resist under the circumstances.

A year before, cutting corners in this respect was alien to everything Ronald Reagan stood for and believed in. However, now the climate around him was different. And he, himself, was not the same man who had had the courage to stand up with forbidding finality and turn his back on a victory that came close but was nonetheless not acceptable.

After weathering an assassination attempt, two operations for cancer, the physical hardship of participating in two presidential campaigns, the debilitating experience of Irangate, and the terrible burdens of seven years in office, at the age of 76, Reagan was not as physically strong or as confident as he had been, even as recently as Reykjavik. Also, Reagan's once formidable team was now diminished by a chief of staff whose congressional background inclined him to seek solutions by compromise.

Then there was the influence of a stronger, more visible, politically powerful and ambitious Nancy. When Nancy told me in September 1987 that the Russians were coming to Washington for a summit some time in the fall, she asked me to pick the best week for them to visit our capital and the best time to sign the Intermediate-range Nuclear Forces Treaty.

"Are you sure everything is all right in the agreement now?" I said.

"Just don't you worry about what's in the treaty," she said. "Ronnie will take care of all that. Your job is to give us the right week for the Russians to come and the best time for signing the agreement."

I did what she asked me to do, but later when Secretary of Defense Caspar Weinberger resigned, I really began to worry. I had always respected Weinberger and felt that his judgment was sound.

It is important to mention that several times that fall the Russians would say they were coming and then back down inexplicably. The negotiations were not running smoothly. Each time there was a false start, I would stay up half the night working on timing the main events and meetings. I tried to do everything I could to insure that the summit would run successfully. Once I remember working nine hours without letup only to be disappointed when the Russians changed their minds.

When I first began to work for Nancy officially, she and I didn't talk as frequently as we did later. Usually we would make a date for the next appointment at the end of the current session. At times, when something would come up unexpectedly, Betsy Bloomingdale acted as liaison between us. I only called Betsy when I needed to contact Nancy in an emergency or when I needed to get back to her at a more convenient time or for some other unanticipated reason.

When Betsy was unavailable, I could call Nancy's social secretary, Elaine Crispin, and leave word that "Joan had called." Once in a great blue moon, I would call the White House switchboard. Routinely they would ask me to leave my number as well as my name before giving the message to Nancy. I was always very firm about never leaving my number or my surname. I knew that switchboard operators everywhere talked and gossiped, and I figured that the White House operators wouldn't be any different.

In September of 1987, Betsy was away from home so much of the time, it was impractical to use her as my liaison. It had reached the point where Nancy and I needed to communicate two and three times a day, so it became necessary to make other arrangements.

Nancy always chided me for refusing to leave my full name and number with the switchboard. I told her it made me uneasy. I told her operators talked. She said I was silly to worry about something like that. "I know," she said, "all White House operators are secretive and reliable."

Nancy told me she would give me an assumed name so that I could always get through to her through the White House switchboard. She would choose the assumed name for me and put it on a list. This would automatically give me access. The name she chose was "Joan Frisco." That really upset me. It was so obviously a made-up name, and "Frisco" is slang for San Francisco.

I reminded her that we were dealing in areas of utmost sensitivity during our phone calls. I remember saying, "Absolute secrecy is imperative." Having the name "Joan Frisco" on the list was not only foolish, it was foolhardy. I argued with her at the time, but she said I was being silly. Looking back on it, I'm sorry I ever agreed. From what happened that fall, I'm now convinced that our conversations were intercepted.

When I think of the hours of work I did, I get mad at myself all over. I should have insisted on an arrangement that was absolutely safe—another reliable intermediary who stayed at home most of the time, someone more easily accessible than Betsy. I see that now. I saw it then. I shouldn't have given in to Nancy.

The minute I learned that the Russians were thinking of coming to a summit in Washington, I set to work. Nancy had asked me to find the best time to sign an agreement. I've never worked so hard on anything in my life. I was working ten- and twelve-hour days. I wanted the chart for the signing of the INF Treaty to be as perfect astrologically as I could make it. The signing time was of the utmost importance. I had October and November to choose from, preferably November.

I gave it a great deal of thought. Despite all the in-depth work

I had done for the Reagans over a six-and-a-half-year period, I knew this was a kind of ultimate responsibility. It was a privilege to be asked, and I gave it the sum of my most measured thought as well as my years of experience in elective astrology. There was so much to keep in mind, I summoned up the sum total of my experience in doing presidential astrology.

First and foremost, I kept in mind the horrible example of the 1985 Inauguration chart. As I've explained, it was a chart that practically insured the danger of assassination and a series of scandals, the worst of which turned out to be Irangate. It was not that I was unaware of these disadvantages when I chose the time. I had been hemmed into it.

President Reagan had to take the oath of office for his second term on January 20, 1985, around mid-day, more or less. There was no possibility of his taking it any other time. I did the very best I could with the chart under the circumstances. I had so little leeway. On the 20th, there was a terrible configuration of the planets Venus, Uranus and Mars which, try as I would, I couldn't eradicate from the Inauguration chart. I could only place it where hopefully it would do the least damage. To erase it had been impossible. This was one of a number of times I would have liked to rearrange the configurations of the planets more to my liking.

I have described this Second Inaugural chart at great length in a previous chapter, but I want to emphasize that when I started out to select a time for the INF Treaty chart, the Inaugural chart was very much in the back of my mind. I wanted above all else to avoid doing what I had been forced to do without an alternative. This time, hopefully, I would be able to choose a satisfactory date within the two-month time period.

When I finally chose my date and time, I was very happy with it. It showed a perfect and lasting agreement between the two parties concerned. It was fair to both sides. Neither side had the advantage. It was a lucky chart. It was very near to perfection.

Above all, I was concerned with the future of this chart. While the basic chart satisfied every requirement, a chart changes or progresses with the passage of time, altering the original circumstances and causing events to happen. The major slow-moving planets advancing as the years passed also would affect it.

I must also explain that when there is only one negative indication in a chart, there may be an undesirable event, but nothing very grave happens. If there are two or more such configurations to the chart, an unfavorable outcome can be expected. This was, as I explained before, the case in the Inauguration chart. What happened was the scandal of Irangate. Above all else, I wanted to make sure that in this most important treaty chart, no two or three negative configurations would occur at the same time or even close to one another.

For hours and hours of painstaking work, I made the mathematical adjustments necessary to insure that no two or three of these configurations would coincide to result in a disaster. I progressed the chart for a hundred years, going over every inch of it, checking and rechecking. Then I proudly presented my finished work to Nancy, i.e., the time to sign the INF Treaty.

The ideal time to sign was on a Sunday. I suggested to Nancy that the summit take place in Washington during the week, to be followed by a visit to the Santa Barbara ranch on the weekend. I was able to do a signing chart for Washington that I could fall back on if the Russians didn't agree to making a California trip, but signing in Santa Barbara was my ideal scenario.

Nancy told Ronnie and Secretary of State George Shultz. She said everybody from Shultz to the State Department on down was making a concerted effort to persuade the Russians to come and sign at the time I'd chosen. She assured me, everybody concerned was doing every conceivable thing they could to make this possible.

The Russians were temperamental about when they would

come. There were several false starts. We thought they would come as planned for a time, but then, they suddenly announced that they would arrive for the summit during the first week in December, take it or leave it.

Nancy called me with the news in early November. She said they were only coming for three working days, that they would arrive on Sunday and have meetings and other official functions and media appearances on Monday, Tuesday and Wednesday. She said I had forty-five minutes to decide on the signing time. After all my careful, patient work, I had less than an hour to make the most important timing decision of my life. I was devastated.

I told Nancy I thought from Gorbachev's chart that they would be most likely to stay over on Thursday. I wanted the signing to take place then, because it was a much better day, quite a good day in fact, but she assured me that it was absolutely set in cement that they would leave early Thursday morning.

Tuesday, December 8th, was a better day than Monday or Wednesday. I had so little time to decide. The chart I came up with was the best I could do under the circumstances.

Like the chart of the time Anthony Kennedy was proposed, this one too had to be timed to perfection. When I told Nancy the time I had chosen, I assumed that she would be even more careful to execute it perfectly than she had been in the case of the Kennedy announcement. The Treaty-signing time being of vastly greater importance, it never occurred to me to double-check that she plan for the Russians to be assembled well in advance. I also assumed she would use the method she had used in the case of Kennedy, beginning early, then stalling the signing until Ronnie received the stopwatch signal.

I see now that I should have called to make sure that everything was done the usual way. Nancy had had her operation for breast cancer on October 17, at a time I chose, about six weeks before the Gorbachevs came.

Nancy's horoscope had indicated to me months in advance that she would develop breast cancer. I didn't want to alarm her by coming right out and telling her. I knew all too well what a worrier she was. So I did what I always do in such cases. I advised her to have monthly checkups and frequent mammograms, certain that the doctors would discover it the minute it developed.

It was discovered in October of 1987, and I chose the time to begin the surgery: 7:37 A.M., October 17th. She was very brave in the way she took it. Nancy never lacked courage. I always admired her for that.

The operation came at the worst time possible—in mid-negotiations for the Washington Summit. She felt that she was needed, and she did what she had to do. She had so much to arrange, she hardly stopped to take time to recover from the operation. She was in a weakened condition for months, with unpleasant side effects. Under such conditions, she can't be blamed for not arranging the signing with her usual forethought and precision.

I was at fault for not having double-checked and reiterated the importance of signing at the precise moment. However, she had her hands so full I didn't want to take up her time, and rather uneasily, I didn't call to remind her again. I assumed that she would arrange this as efficiently as she'd always done. At any rate, she didn't.

I chose the time of 1:48 P.M. for President Ronald Reagan and Secretary General Mikhail Gorbachev to sign the INF Treaty. Because the day I was forced to use was not ideal, the time I chose needed to be as precise as the choice for the announcement of Anthony Kennedy's nomination to the Supreme Court. I had told Nancy to assemble everyone concerned by 1:30, and that was cutting it close. As it was, the Gorbachevs arrived late; they took their time seating themselves and insisted on posing for endless photographs to satisfy the media. The actual signing time was 2:01:59 P.M. on December 8, 1987, about fourteen minutes later than the time I had chosen.

The execution of the INF Treaty signing time was flawed. The exact time I had asked for would have had the effect of filling a teacup nearly to the brim, at the same time insuring that the teacup would not fill up too fast and spill over.

What we now had, in effect, was a car whose brakes had failed, speeding unchecked through crowded intersections. But if one views it more optimistically, it had the potential of being like a thoroughbred racing unchallenged toward the finish line. I must admit I didn't know which of these two possibilities was in effect when I witnessed the haste with which Congress confirmed the INF Treaty. I didn't know whether to be heartsick or to rejoice.

In addition to asking me to choose the vital signing time in the space of an hour, Nancy also gave me one more hour to choose the other times when the meetings, the banquets and media interviews would be held. It had taken me ten or twelve hours to do this on the other occasions when the Russians had backed out at the last minute. I told Nancy to let the chips fall where they may. Not only was I too tired by then, but even had I been rested and fresh, choosing nine or ten times that fast was an impossibility.

As it turned out, I had been right about the Russians staying on for Thursday. On Thursday, had the signing time been less precise, it wouldn't have mattered so vitally. It could have been off as much as fifteen or twenty minutes on that day.

During his days in Washington, Gorbachev made a very favorable impression. The media went all out for him. Ronnie, himself, was somewhat eclipsed, which I don't think would have happened had I had the time and strength to plan for him as I usually did.

It was natural for Gorbachev to be well received in the United States. With his Aquarian Mercury, the American people would naturally respond to him and he to them. He had the potential in his birth chart of thinking more like an American than a Russian.

To this day, I don't know how safe that treaty is for us or for the world. I haven't the heart to progress that signing chart as I did the other. But I do know one thing absolutely. When what is planned is not meant to be, something will happen to delay the beginning time to a time more descriptive of the actual event and how it will turn out in the long run.

The lamented "perfect time" I chose in the latter part of November was not meant to be. Not even the next best time could be executed perfectly. In itself this is the answer.

A number of journalists have speculated that the Russians were listening in to Nancy's and my conversations. I wouldn't be at all surprised. Proper precautions were not taken to prevent this. I was afraid of it at the time. What I had feared probably happened.

No doubt this explains why the Russians didn't agree to come at the better time that would have benefited both sides equally. Perhaps they didn't believe an American astrologer would be evenhanded. Perhaps they wanted the advantage. Whatever the reason, things happened when and how they did. Fate took a hand, "and all your piety and wit cannot cancel out one line of it."

## The Moscow Summit

Nancy asked me to give her the best time for the Moscow Summit early in 1988. She told me the Russians were being indefinite and that it was hard to pin them down.

My scenario, and it wasn't ideal by a long way, was early May. However, the Soviets, who had, in the final analysis, called the shots on their visit to Washington, now decreed that the Moscow Summit would take place in late May.

It was a horrendous time astrologically, and I said so. I've rarely seen worse general configurations of the planets. I remember after it was known that I had been doing the Reagans' astrology, one of the more serious news programs had asked an astrologer to comment on the timing of the Moscow Summit. He replied, "She had to have had a frontal lobotomy to have chosen such a time." I was terribly embarrassed to have anyone who knew anything whatsoever about astrology believe for one moment that I had chosen that time.

When the Reagans told me about the week the summit was to be held, I searched for a safe time for them to take off from Washington, a time that would guarantee that the summit would go reasonably well. There was only one possible time. Again I employed the method I had used for the Kennedy announcement. Although a camel going through a needle's eye would have had an easier task, I finally produced a viable trip chart. It was earlier than the people planning the schedule had requested, but May 25, 1988, at 10:30 A.M. was the time I chose for Air Force One to take off from Andrews Air Force Base.

It turned out to be better than the time the White House staff were thinking of originally. My time allowed the Reagans a brief respite in Finland to recover from jet lag. This also allowed them to schedule a meeting with the President of Finland that couldn't have taken place otherwise.

It required all my ingenuity to find a time to start the trip. As was usual with all the summits, Nancy consulted me about any information I could give her on the scheduled meetings and appearances. She gave me a list of these before I left on my Mediterranean cruise in April, and I was to get back to her with the usual briefing upon returning.

As it turned out, that briefing never took place. Nancy never called me after I refused to ignore the media when the Regan book came out. *Time* magazine asked me to comment, meeting by meeting and appearance by appearance, on the Moscow Summit from the astrological point of view, but I begged off, saying that I would need to use the exact times. I had them, but they had been given to me in confidence. In addition, I felt it was inappropriate for me to comment under the circumstances.

I would like to go on record about something of major importance that was done for all the wrong reasons and against my best advice. Before I left for the Mediterranean, I only had the chance to analyze one of the times Nancy submitted to me for the week in Moscow. It was June 1, 2:00 P.M., when the ratification documents for the Intermediate-range Nuclear Forces Treaty were to be signed. I told her it was a horrible time. She assured me that the signing was of no importance, just a few insignificant details. But I said, "If the paper contains anything of the slightest importance, don't do it."

The last advice that I ever gave Nancy was sound as the Rock of Gibraltar astrologically. I said, "Go to Moscow if you will. The time I have chosen will guarantee a safe journey. Enjoy your global photo-opportunity, the hands reaching out, the adulation, but for God's sake, don't sign anything of importance at 2:00 P.M. on June 1 in Moscow. I'm warning you, signing anything of importance at that time is 'Roosevelt at Yalta' stuff."

I knew Ronnie wanted to be remembered always as having cemented the historic arms reduction agreement by appearing in Moscow. It was only human for him to wish to do so. "But please, don't sign anything at that meeting," I pleaded with Nancy. "Leave something for the next person. Ronnie has done enough. His place in history is already enviable."

Even now, looking at the chart of the signing in Moscow makes me physically ill. I can only hope what was signed was of minor importance, "just insignificant details," as Nancy had said during our last formal consultation.

The following is an excerpt from President Reagan's speech to

soviet cultural and artistic figures today, and from his speech to
students at Moscow State University and a question-and-answer
session with them:

> Your generation is living in one of the most exciting,
> hopeful times in Soviet history.
> I am reminded of the famous passage near the end of
> Gogol's *Dead Souls*, comparing his nation to a speeding
> troika. Gogol asks, "What will be its destination?" But he
> writes, "There was no answer, save the bell pouring forth a
> marvelous sound."
> . . . In this Moscow spring, this May 1988, we may be
> allowed that hope, that freedom, like the fresh green
> sapling planted over Tolstoy's grave, will blossom forth at
> last in the rich fertile soil of your people and culture. We
> may be allowed to hope that the marvelous sound of a new
> openness will keep rising through, ringing through, lead-
> ing to a new world of reconciliation, friendship and peace.

Strolling through Red Square together like two old friends
toward the end of the Moscow Summit, Reagan and Gorbachev
attracted a crowd of well-wishers. Someone in the crowd thrust
a child before Gorbachev, who picked up the youngster and
with a broad smile urged him to shake hands with "Grandfather
Reagan." Reagan reached out his hands and cuddled the child.

CBS White House correspondent, Bill Plante, emerged from
the attendant press corps and asked President Reagan:

"Do you still think that the U.S.S.R. is an 'Evil Empire'?"

Pausing as if he had pondered that question before, the
President slowly replied in a single word: "No."

# Afterthoughts

Throughout history, only the bravest (or the very foolish) have attempted to alter the status quo. Jesus threw the money changers out of the temple. There were Socrates, Lincoln, Gandhi, Martin Luther King, Jr., and many others.

Prometheus, a hero of Greek mythology, defied the gods to bring fire to man. His reward was a punishment. He was chained to a rock for all eternity with an eagle pecking at his liver. What Prometheus did and what happened to him is a myth with a message, a commentary on human resistance to change.

I don't think for one minute that Gorbachev is foolhardy. He's a practical man of action. He has proved that. He is also a man of great vision. He has proved that, too. He has more courage than any living political leader now in power. That is why I admire him most—for his courage.

When Gorbachev took over, Soviet society had been frozen solid like a block of ice for the better part of a century. Now, only four and a half years after the Geneva Summit, during which President Reagan suggested that economic and political liberalization would benefit the Russian people, the once solid block is cracking in places and thawing and melting down. Even as I write, thousands of people are flooding and overflowing the Berlin Wall barrier, demanding freedom and unity between East and West Germany. There is democratization in Poland. At last, in the once doomed Eastern block countries, millions have hope.

Within the borders of the Soviet Union, within the Eastern Block satellite nations, glasnost and perestroika have made a difference. But the resistance to change inside the U.S.S.R. is a formidable challenge, even to a man of Gorbachev's powerful capabilities. I can only pray for him. If he goes and the military establishment replaces him, all that has been set in motion will be lost, and we will be more at risk because of Reagan's and Gorbachev's daring. I only hope George Bush will deal with the Soviets cautiously and wisely.

Looking ahead, I know I may one day regret my part in preparing the President for Geneva. I had hoped that Gorbachev's vision of peace, like Reagan's, could lead to a world where some day war would be obsolete. President Gorbachev is dedicated to the ideal that peace is possible. But will Gorbachev remain in power? That is critical.

From my analysis, Mikhail Gorbachev will be tested over and over, almost beyond endurance. If he can survive these testing periods, he will emerge stronger than ever. If not, people looking back on the 1980s will tell the tale of two men who tried to bring world peace by disarming unilaterally.

Perhaps Reagan and Gorbachev will be remembered in world history with the same spirit I remember the story of that lone British soldier who risked his life to make a peace offering to his enemy at Christmas during World War I. And remembering these two leaders as I remembered him, someone will try again, because peace on earth cannot be denied mankind forever. Most of mankind is longing for peace on earth.

# Appendix

# Modern Astrology

Modern astrology is an analytic and predictive discipline, based on the accepted modern science of astronomy in the same way a medical diagnosis is supported by laboratory reports and economic forecasts result from statistical analyses.

Like all other modern scientific disciplines, astrology has many branches:

*Natal*: This tells about an individual's character, the kind of person he will develop into and the sort of experiences he will have during his life; also the external forces that will aid and hinder him.

*Synastry*: The comparison of two people's horoscopes to determine how they will get along in general and at various future times and what will be the outcome of their relationship.

*Horary*: The astrologer gives you the answer to a question based on the time you ask it.

*Elective*: The astrologer selects a time for you to begin a project such as an important trip, a conference, a speech, a document signing, the start of a business, marriage, a move into a home, surgery and so on. Hopefully, the astrologer is able to insure the desired outcome or a favorable result. It is also possible to bring two people into agreement when political arm-twisting is necessary.

*Mundane*: A consideration of charts such as Ingresses and Equinoxes, great conjunctions and cycle charts of planets for various locations. The astrologer can chart the horoscopes of cities and countries when the time of their inception is known. This also includes prediction of earthquakes, hurricanes and other natural disasters. Some mundane astrologers also specialize in predicting the weather.

*Location*: This is of utmost importance. Some events are fated to happen to you wherever you are. But more often than not, locations makes a difference in a person's life. For instance, what may happen to you in New York during a certain time period can be different from what would happen to you if you were in Tokyo at that same time. Some places are also generally more fortunate for an individual than others.

*Financial*: Prediction of taxes, stock market action, currencies, areas of the economy that will be strong or weak. Unemployment. Taxation. Debts.

*Medical*: A consideration of important health matters and times of illness and vulnerability to disease or other health problems.

A political astrologer makes use of all of the charts described above.

### The Basic Components of a Natal Chart

The natal, or birth, chart is the most fundamental form of astrology. It is based on the time and place of birth, the time

consisting of the date, month, year and exact time of day the
infant inhales his or her first breath.

The horoscope wheel looks like a pie divided into twelve
pieces. Each of these pieces represents a department of the
individual's life. The First house, called the rising sign, or the
ascendant, represents the person himself, his psychological
characteristics and physical body; the Second house, his money
and personal possessions of value; the Third house, his brothers
and sisters, his teachers, weekend trips, his practical mind and
interest in books or reading; the Fourth house, his mother, his
home, the beginning and end of his life; the Fifth house,
children, pleasures and amusements, courtship, social life; the
Sixth, health and illness, small animals, work that is done in an
inferior capacity where the individual is not his own boss; the
Seventh, the marriage or business partner or open enemies; the
Eighth, generative sex, death, the partner's money; the Ninth,
travel, government, the law, publicity, publishing, religion or
philosophy, fame; the Tenth house, the father, the profession if
the person works for himself or is the head of a family or
business. The Tenth house also describes one's prestige and
worldly standing. The Eleventh house represents friends, hopes
and wishes, organizations and clubs; the Twelfth house, the
past, obscurity, hospital, prisons, isolation, secret sorrows, the
interior world of the subconscious mind, the creative imagina-
tion or the world of drugs and hallucinogens.

In political astrology, the houses have added significance. In
the chart of a political leader, the First house is still the leader
himself, but the Second often has to do with his country's
finances and treasury; the Third, newspapers, reporters, short
journeys; the Fourth, the property of his constituents, the opposition party to the party in power; the Fifth, his own popularity
and the stock market; the Sixth, employment or unemployment, government workers, the military, the police and all
uniformed services; the Seventh house, the public, open ene-

mies or other countries opposed to the country in an actual war; the Eighth, the death rate, taxes, and war casualties; the Ninth, the judiciary, the church, foreign travel or other long journeys, and foreign affairs; the Tenth, the public standing and position of authority he or she occupies; the Eleventh, legislative bodies; and the Twelfth, dependent people, such as the homeless or those on welfare or in hospitals or prisons, and scandal and disgrace and, very importantly, assassins and others who operate secretly.

In the chart of a country or city, these houses can be interpreted in the same way as that of a political leader except that the First house represents the people, and the Fourth house, the weather or natural disasters, such as earthquakes, tornadoes, drought, etc.; the Tenth house represents the president, premier or prime minister of a country, the mayor of a city or any other, the chief executive of the government.

During May 1988, when it became known that I had done Presidential astrology professionally, there was a good deal of confusion in the public mind about what I had done. A great many people thought of astrology in terms of the Sun Signs columns I mentioned before. Pop astrologers make themselves very visible, like showmen or entertainers of sorts. Primarily they deal in terms of Sun Signs. The reason this is done is that the Sun is in approximately the same sign on the same day in any year except, of course, when your Sun is "on the cusp," which refers to the time the Sun is leaving one sign and entering the next sign of the Zodiac. In an accurate horoscope, this has to be calculated exactly on the day of the changeover in the specific year for one to know which sign the person's Sun is actually in. For pop astrology, all you have to know is your birthday, nothing more. This is a vast oversimplification as you will see.

For an accurate and complete horoscope, one must take into consideration not only the Sun but the Moon and the eight planets, with special emphasis on the planets connected with the ascendant, or rising sign, which is based on the time of birth. Each planet must be found in one of the twelve signs of the Zodiac, and each is also placed in one of the twelve houses.

In an individual's birth chart, each of the ten planets (this includes the Sun and the Moon) can be in any sign of the Zodiac. In some charts, each planet may be in a different sign of the Zodiac, while in other charts, the planets may be concentrated in only a few signs. It all depends on the position of the planets at the time and place of birth of the individual. To see how this works, pay particular attention to the Mars description in Reagan's and Roosevelt's horoscope below.

The personal planets, or the faster-moving planets, are the Sun, the Moon, Mercury, Venus, Mars, Jupiter and Saturn. These planets are the only ones astronomers, as well as astrologers, knew about until Uranus, Neptune, and Pluto were discovered between the end of the 18th century and 1930.

Please refer to my book *Astrology for Adults* for the description of the Sun, Moon and planets in the Zodiacal signs. In this book, I also mention the configurations, or aspects, of the planets, which are their relationship to one another in the birth chart. These can be favorable or unfavorable. When I speak of the transiting of a planet, I refer to the way a planet moving currently through the heavens relates to the individual's chart.

*The Sun.* The Sun represents the individuality, the self you feel behind the handshake. All the planets revolve around the Sun and reflect its light, so a strong Sun is absolutely essential for the success of any leader. In a political chart, it represents the person as an authority figure. The weak position of Dukakis's Sun showed that he never would be a world leader.

*The Moon.* This represents the personality, the way your mother treated you as a child, the women in your life. In a politician's chart, it is very important, as it indicates his public image. Reagan's Moon is in Taurus, the best and most conservative sign for the Moon. The Moon has the fastest cycle of any heavenly body that directly affects us; it goes through every sign of the Zodiac in approximately 27½ days, or a lunar month.

*Mercury*. This represents how your mind works, your voice, your ability to communicate with others in writing or speech, the ability to think and formulate plans.

*Venus*. This represents what someone is like in a love relationship. With a politician it is quite important as an indication of public popularity, in contrast with a private individual, whose Venus is mainly concerned with his love life and personal happiness.

*Mars*. This represents forcefulness in action, athletic ability, sex appeal. It is tremendously important in a political figure's chart because it describes the ability to lead and put plans across. To be successful, military men as well as executives of every sort must have a strong Mars. Usually Mars is strongest in Capricorn or Aries. Ronald Reagan's Mars combines both of these strengths. It is in the sign of Capricorn, its exaltation or the strongest sign for Mars to be in. It is also in the First house, which is the equivalent of its being in Aries, the first sign of the Zodiac, in which Mars is most at home. This shows the ability to put into effect the grand strategies Reagan conceived with his practical Capricorn Mercury and the great leadership ability to put these plans into effect.

It is interesting to note that the Roosevelt's Mars was in Gemini, not ordinarily a strong sign for Mars to be placed in. In his case, however, his leadership ability was phenomenal. Gemini, Mercury's sign, is a sign having to do both with speech and the air waves of radio. And the strength of Roosevelt's leadership stemmed from speeches on radio in his inimitable voice and with his patrician accent. His "Fireside Chats" calmed people's fears during the Depression and gave them the confidence to survive. With his "Day of Infamy" speech, he led the country into war. The placement of his Mars in his Tenth house, which resembles the tenth sign of Capricorn, is tremendously strong.

*Jupiter.* This is the planet of luck, good financial judgment, religion and philosophy. It also gives a genial, confident, optimistic nature and salesmanship ability (so essential for any politician to be able to influence opinion and inspire people to have confidence in him).

*Saturn.* This is the planet of hardship, burdens, obstacles and heavy responsibilities. However, Saturn, which rules the skeleton of the human body, gives backbone and the strength of character to take on responsibility. Reagan's Saturn is in Taurus. Many great generals, such as Ulysses S. Grant, had this position, which gives the ability to plan great military strategies.

The planets just described have been known to astronomers and astrologers since ancient times. However, there were three additional planets moving through the signs of the Zodiac more slowly than the seven I have just mentioned which had an effect on human life even though they were quite unknown until 1781, when Uranus was the first slower-moving, or outer, planet to be discovered.

When I describe what Uranus means in an individual's horoscope and how it acts as it transits (moves) through the Zodiac and affects an individual's chart, you will be able to understand why astrologers were dealing with incomplete data at the end of the 17th century, when astrology began to be debunked.

*Uranus.* Uranus, discovered in 1781 by Sir William Herschel, governs personal charisma. If it is well placed in a chart, it gives a strong inner will and the personal magnetism to inspire and to lead. Hitler's Uranus was rising, and his hysterical speech patterns, which led an entire nation into a kind of insanity, are typical of Uranus at its most powerful and its worst. At best, Uranus gives genius, the ability to invent and an understanding of all kinds of gadgets and machinery. It is the planet which had to do with music and sound and noise. In extreme cases, it is so determined and aggressive as to be sadistic.

When the transit (movement) of Uranus relates unfavorably to a person's horoscope, it has a very upsetting and unsettling effect. It causes unexpected hostile behavior on the part of other people, or the person's own behavior becomes erratic and irrational. Sudden upheaval, accidents and disasters occur.

Uranus is both a kingmaker and a throne-toppler. As it progresses through the signs of the Zodiac and affects people's planets, it has the power to raise an individual up to the very heights of prominence and power practically overnight or to cast him down to ignominy, obscurity, poverty or disgrace. It can cause death by assassination, as in the case of John F. Kennedy. It can cause sudden attractions and sudden breakups or divorce. What is broken up by an adverse Uranus transit, like Humpty Dumpty can never be mended. Yet even the apparent disasters Uranus causes have the merit of removing dead wood from our lives. Usually its action is so traumatic, however, it is hard to understand such side benefits at the time.

It is hard to take precautions against Uranus; its action is sudden and unexpected and impossible to oppose or prevent. There is nothing to do but live through it somehow, if you are able to, until its malefic power is spent. It was a two-year transit of Uranus to the most important degree of Nixon's horoscope that caused Watergate and his eventual resignation from the presidency in disgrace. At worst, Uranus can cause total destruction and maim you for life, physically or psychologically, or worse. The message Uranus gives the powerful is that "a pebble can overturn the chariot of a King," as when a shot fired at Sarajevo by a virtually unknown person killed Archduke Ferdinand, and gave the excuse for starting World War I and caused the death of millions.

You can see why astrologers who were unaware that Uranus was operating in the heavens must have been baffled when they could not account entirely for what was going on in their clients' incomplete charts. And you can also understand why, with this new discovery, astrology that didn't take Uranus into consideration began to be debunked.

*Neptune.* The existence of Neptune was first predicted in 1846 by the mathematical calculations of the French astronomer Urbain Jean Joseph Leverrier. That same year, Johann Gottfried Galle, a German astronomer, discovered Neptune within one degree of the position Leverrier had described. Neptune is the planet of illusions. A perfect example is theatrical lighting or *trompe l'oeil* or Impressionist art. Neptune specializes in things not being in their natural order. People with Neptune prominent in their charts like to masquerade or pretend to be other than they are. Often they put on too much makeup or indulge in other fantasies. In a larger sense, Neptune in favorable configuration to the other planets produces the purest, most idealistic people, while its unfavorable aspects result in depths of degradation and corruption.

The Neptunian quite typically never wants things to be the way they are and often wants to be out of the world while he is in it, so that often these people resort to drug or alcohol abuse. These people are to be found at the top of the tree or among society's most degraded and destitute.

Neptunians are distinct individuals who stand out from the crowd. They always have great charm, in some cases sincere, in others, insincere. They have sensitive, finely organized nervous systems. They tend to be masochistic in contrast to Uranians, who, while just as individual, are more aggressive and positive. Certain combinations of Neptune and Uranus in an individual's chart make for a very contradictory and complex character, often perverse.

Usually the things represented by the sign Neptune is in are romanticized, often unrealistically. Women born during the first decade and a half of this century when Neptune was in the sign of Cancer (the Moon sign so representative of the feminine principle and most especially motherhood), not only idealized their own mothers, but later romanticized the mothering they lavished on their own children.

In political astrology Neptune represents fraud, scandal, false testimony and lies as well as other forms of deception, dishonesty and trickery. In financial matters, Neptune represents schemes, swindles and bubbles that burst, inflation, wild speculation, as well as spies and assassins and common thieves. Neptune is also responsible for leaks and rumors from unidentified sources that cannot be traced.

*Pluto.* Pluto was discovered in 1930 at the Lowell Observatory in Flagstaff, Arizona. Aptly named for the god of the underworld in Greek mythology, it came to astronomers' attention at a time when gangsters were organizing and dictators were on the rise. It represents all things that are mass-produced endlessly and automatically. It is also the planet of the media; when it affects a politician's horoscope adversely, there might be a savaging by the media which was the case when Pluto afflicted a sensitive degree in Dan Quayle's horoscope after he was nominated for the Vice-Presidency in August and during September of 1988. With a good Pluto aspect, on the other hand, the media can give a politician or entertainer a real boost. Pluto also governs partisans and lobbyists and groups that form to counteract what another group is doing. Media figures usually have Pluto prominently placed in their charts.

These three most recently discovered planets have a great deal to do with modern life. They are always prominent in the charts of 20th-century leaders, and when their movements through the Zodiac effect a politician's horoscope for good or ill, they have a major effect.

It takes Uranus seven years to go through a single sign of the Zodiac; Neptune takes fourteen years, and Pluto between thirteen and thirty-five. Neptune and Pluto affect whole generations, and Uranus, sub-generations; a study of their progression through the signs of the Zodiac would enable one to write the history of the world. It is curious to note, for instance, that syphilis came into being during the Hundred Years War, when Neptune and Pluto were in Scorpio, the sign of sex, just as AIDS came into being first when Neptune progressed through Scorpio, followed now by Pluto.

Uranus upsets the areas ruled by the sign it is in. Neptune idealizes them and creates illusions and deceptions regarding them. Pluto overthrows the matters ruled by the sign it is in. The Pluto in Leo generation, who made themselves felt in the early Sixties, were rebels who tried to overthrow Leo authority, for instance.

Like the Pluto of mythology, who spent half the time above and half below Earth, people with Pluto in the most visible part of their charts, the Tenth house of profession, have their professional life run smoothly for a period and then, as if by some sort of magic faucet, turn off. An on-again, off-again action is typical of Pluto in whatever department of life it is found. It is like a two-sided coin—the head and tail of life. Pluto rules the people who must flee their native land and start life anew in an alien country.

### Progressing a Natal Chart

An astrologer brings a natal chart up to date yearly for the average client. He or she uses relative times to do this. For instance, by one method, every day after birth equals a year of an individual's life; by another method, approximately four minutes equals a year. When progressing the Moon, about two hours equals a month.

The birth chart contains in it every indication of an individual's physical, emotional, mental and spiritual development, as well as everything he is meant to experience on a personal level. An event is rather like a mole in the human body. It is there from birth, but it may make an appearance later in life. Few people experience everything their horoscopes indicate to be possible. They don't live that intensely or conscientiously or take advantage of all their opportunities the way remarkable achievers do. For this reason, Presidents' charts are easier to read. I did the President's chart hourly and daily and weekly in addition to the monthly and yearly predictions I did for other clients.

## The Transits, or Weather Conditions, of Life

The faster-moving planets change positions almost daily. The slower ones stay in the same place for a longer time period and have a longer-lasting effect. All of them describe external conditions. These can be fatalistic and impossible to avoid, especially the transits (movements) of Uranus, Saturn, Pluto and sometimes Neptune. These planets make a considerable difference when their movements relate to sensitive points in an individual's horoscope.

Jupiter transits can be good, but you have to respond to them by taking advantage of the opportunities presented. Uranus and Pluto, when configurating a horoscope adversely, can have dramatic ill effects. They can describe an assassination attempt, a car or plane accident, an individual or group's turning against you, or the individuals in your home environment suddenly turning hostile. In contrast, Neptune transits are hazier and less clearly defined. They resemble a slow-spreading cancer. You don't discover the harm Neptune is doing until after it is too late. Neptune is an insidious planet; if he starts rumors about you, he does so behind your back. One is rarely aware that anything is happening when Neptune is doing his worst.

When the transiting Mars joins a slower-moving planet or planets to make an adverse configuration to a horoscope, it is an ominous sign. When it does this alone, one can suffer cuts and bruises, falls, burns or other more or less serious accidents, depending on the chart. Sometimes these external conditions can cause internal changes and suffering. Bad transits, like bad weather, can bring on colds or arthritis or allergies, and can lower your resistance to contagious diseases. They can also trigger depression or other mental disturbances.

In a national leader's chart, terrible interior suffering as well as political damage can occur when, in the case of adverse Pluto, pressure groups combine, media forces unite, or countries, as in time of great wars, conspire to turn against him. Or, in the case of Uranus, a strong individual comes out of nowhere to lead others to attack him by surprise.

The transit of Saturn are fated and unavoidable for everyone. Saturn exacts a full price and to the last penny. It teaches each of us our hardest lessons; the greater the man, the greater price Saturn exacts.

During fortunate periods, on the other hand, all these major planets can converge to favor a leader and further his aims.

## What an Astrologer Is Able to Contribute

Before an astrologer advises a client, and this is true of Presidents as well as others, she must decide which events she can improve upon, which dangers can be averted, and which difficult situations are absolutely fated and unavoidable and must be lived through.

An astrologer can anticipate danger in a horoscope and deliver a timely warning. He or she can make a good period better by predicting it is safe to go forward. With the added advantage of skillful timing, an astrologer can provide invaluable help. How-

ever, when an astrologer is certain that a difficult period is
unavoidable, when there is no way to deter or prevent it, all he
or she can do is to comfort the client and encourage him or her
to live through it with the most philosophical, positive and
constructive attitude. That was no doubt what Nancy meant in
her book when she said I comforted her.

I often take my clients' minds off of present frustrations by
suggesting that they use a time of danger or stalemate to lie low
and make preparations for better times ahead. I find it helps
people going through an unusually stressful period to know
when and how it will end. I did this for Nancy many times
during her years as First Lady, and you saw in the Irangate
chapter how I also helped the President.

## Timing

### *The Meaning of a Moment in Time*

One of an astrologer's most important functions is timing. The
time chosen to undertake a project determines its exact nature,
events along the way and hazards to be avoided as the project
unfolds. Most importantly, it tells whether the project will end
in failure or achieve success.

Timing is a creative act. It is based on conceptual thinking. It
requires technical skills. One must have years of experience in
addition to natural talent to do it really well. Excellence in
timing requires patience and planning, and the willingness to
explore every conceivable possibility and to take infinite pains.

A great sculptor must visualize the finished figure before he
can free that figure from the marble. A great timer must visualize the nature of an event and the outcome he desires before he
can select an appropriate moment from the steady flow of time.
The timer is limited by the nature of the moments available and

his skill in extracting them, just as a sculptor is limited by the size and the shape of the marble and his artistry. Not even a Michelangelo can carve a six-foot statue from a four-foot block of marble. Nor can the greatest astrologer make something happen that is not meant to be.

Once the time is selected, the astrologer must point out its imperfections and tell the client what to look out for so that nothing foreseeable can prevent the successful outcome of the venture he has timed.

### Presidential Timing

When a political leader desires a favorable outcome for something he has decided to begin, ideally he describes in detail to his astrologer what he would like to accomplish.

### Is it possible for this person to do such a thing?

The first thing the astrologer has to decide is whether or not it is possible for the client to do something successfully. For instance, if a young Peggy Fleming had asked me to select a time for her to become the Heavyweight Champion of the World or Muhammad Ali wished to win an Olympic Gold in ice skating, I would have had to turn them down. An astrologer is not a magician. There are always limitations. An astrologer must select a time that accords with the horoscope of the individual consulting him.

### Is it possible at this time?

Sometimes what the person wants to do is possible, but not at the time he wishes. The person has to wait. For instance, there was no way I could have found a suitable time for Ronald Reagan to win the Presidency in 1976. It was absolutely denied at that time by a movement of the planet Saturn in relation to his birth chart.

*How astrology seizes the moment and insures success.*

Choosing an appropriate time for an important beginning is normally the most difficult task an astrologer performs. Once in a while, it can be done easily, but that is the exception. Unimportant times can be arrived at more quickly because they do not need to be perfect. Important times must be as near to perfection as the limits imposed by circumstances allow. Other astrologers have told me they wouldn't be bothered to consider all the ramifications of a single problem as exhaustively as I do. But I am a perfectionist at heart; I can't help taking pains.

When I was beginning to learn how to do such charts, I would spend several months of effort on a single chart, and the client would have to wait until his project could be started at a nearly perfect time, perhaps as long as a year or two. I would pore over my books for hours, debating with myself the merits of one time or another.

Years of diligent practice resulted in the development of certain skills: I can see complex configurations at a glance, and I can choose a time for less important matters relatively fast.

While I didn't realize it then, I was preparing to choose important times for President Reagan, some of them crucial. No time chosen for a President is unimportant. There is always the necessity for safety. But some events, such as the declaration to run for a second term, the taking of an oath of office, the delivery of the State of the Union message, the trips to the Geneva and Reykjavik Summit, the INF Treaty signing, or undergoing an operation for cancer are of utmost importance, and many of them had to be done on a day that was not of my own choosing or with time limitations outside of my control.

Sometimes, I had weeks or months to plan; sometimes I had to make important choices in a matter of hours.

Less important times, such as a presidential speechmaking trip when he could leave in the morning and return later that same day, were relatively easy. But of course, even those had to be safe. With a one-day excursion that had to be done during a certain month or two-week period, when there were no major impediments, I could choose a departure time relatively easily. But often when I had to do this within time limits, I would warn Nancy of hazards to look out for, such as my cautioning her to have the microphone checked before Reagan's September 2, 1980, debate with John Anderson in Baltimore. I chose the time for their private plane to take off from Washington the day of the debate, and because I had chosen it, I knew exactly what to look out for.

Presidential astrology has its advantages. The President can often command that things be done at a certain time in a way other people cannot. And he has the very great advantage of having Air Force One at his disposal at all times. When I am doing such technical, in-depth work for a client, naturally it is an advantage for him to have a private plane. The takeoff time of commercial planes is too unreliable these days, and the times I set are always very exact.

Also, I have an indicator which enables me to tell what may happen to someone practically minute by munute. I have my own way of doing this, and believe me, it is so time-consuming, I wouldn't dream of doing it in such detail for anyone except a President—perhaps I should say for President Ronald Reagan. I would never do astrology for a President again. The over seven years of work I did was incredibly demanding. The work for the President had to come ahead of everything else. It was always uppermost in my mind. When I ceased to do it, I must say, I breathed a sigh of relief.

## ACKNOWLEDGMENTS

My grateful thanks to my mother, the late Zelda Quigley, for introducing me to astrology and to both her and my father, the late John Baird Quigley, for their love and example throughout my life. I would also like to thank them and my sister, Ruth, for their discretion and encouragement during the Reagan years and thanks also to Ruth for her advice concerning this book.

My gratitude to my teacher, the late Mrs. Jerome J. Pearson, who taught me astrology, and to my dear friend and valued colleague in astrology, Ivy Jacobson.

I would like to thank Ruth Freeman Solomon for her friendship and assistance throughout my literary career and for her invaluable advice.

I would like to thank Dr. Albert Shumate for all his kindness, encouragement and advice.

My thanks to astrologer Nicki Michaels for her loyalty, friendship and the excellence of her computer work.

My gratitude to Joyce Jansen who not only has been my agent but contributed her research assistance to this project.

I am grateful to my publisher Hillel Black for his faith in me and in this book and his editorial help.

Others who have contributed meaningfully include: Paul Grell, Betty Gardiner, Henry Donahue, Mrs. M.L. Cohn, Putnam Livermore, Salvador Bonilla and Linda Witt.

# Index